Jesse Jackson & the Politics of Charisma

The Rise and Fall of the PUSH/Excel Program

Ernest R. House.

Westview Press / BOULDER & LONDON

For "Mom," my grandmother Nellie Maud White,
whose acts of spirit and redemption
so affected all our lives

Copyright © 1988 by Westview Press, Inc.

Published in 1988 in the United States of America by Westview Press, Inc., 5500 Central Avenue, Boulder, Colorado 80301

Library of Congress Cataloging-in-Publication Data
House, Ernest R.
  Jesse Jackson and the politics of charisma: the rise and fall of
the PUSH/Excel program / Ernest R. House.
    p.   cm.
  Bibliography: p.
  Includes index.
  ISBN 0-8133-0767-8
  1. Jackson, Jesse, 1941–   2. Operation Push.   3. Afro
-Americans—Education.   I. Title.
E840.8.J35H68 1988
973.92'092'4—dc19   88-14362
                                                              CIP

Printed and bound in the United States of America

The paper used in this publication meets the requirements of the American National Standard for Permanence of Paper for Printed Library Materials Z39.48-1984.

6   5   4   3   2   1

Jesse Jackson & the Politics of Charisma

Contents

A Moral Order, *123*
Crowd Emotion and the Use of Rhetoric, *125*
Institutionalization of Crowd Emotion, *126*
Deliverance from Oppression, *127*
Our Time Has Come, *129*

Preface

On January 15, 1975, the Reverend Jesse Jackson was leading a demonstration around the White House to protest the lack of jobs for black youths. As the demonstrators marched, Jackson was shocked to discover that many of the black youths marching with him were drunk or on drugs, many of them "out of control." Abruptly, he called a halt to the demonstration and sent the marchers home.

Within a few months, Jackson launched a national campaign in the urban high schools of the nation to save the black youths of his country, to get them off drugs and motivate them to work hard, study in school, develop self-discipline, and become successful in American society. A program called PUSH for Excellence, or PUSH/Excel, was an outgrowth of his Operation PUSH organization. Society had no solutions for the black teenagers whom Jackson was trying to help, and his efforts were highly praised, at first, by the media and government officials.

Jackson's moral campaign was highlighted by the mass media in front-page newspaper coverage and prime-time television. "Jesse Jackson's Crusade," the media called it. Within a few months, Jackson had raised funds from private sources to support the effort, and within a few years, at the direct intervention of Hubert Humphrey, who was dying of cancer, he was offered substantial financial support from the federal government. School districts lined up to implement the new program, and government and school officials at all levels, it seemed, were willing to help.

After only three more years of effort, the program was in a shambles; the mass media that had lauded it only a short time before now proclaimed it a failure. Jackson himself was accused of various misdeeds and chastised for his demagoguery and lack of follow-through. Jackson defended himself by asserting that his political enemies had sabotaged the effort. Shortly afterward, he put the PUSH/Excel program behind him and went on to become a candidate for the presidency of the United States. The black youths he had tried to help were in even more desperate trouble than before. What had gone wrong? How could something so promising end in such failure? Lots of explanations, mostly accusations, were attempted at the time, but they contradicted one another.

In this book I attempt to describe the events and analyze why they occurred. As one might expect, the events are complex, convoluted, and are not simple to grasp. They form a classic case of racial politics American-style, a drama of misunderstandings and mistrust, of accusations and suspicions, of good intentions turned sour, of soaring aspirations, and of equally steep disillusionment.

There were three major actors in this drama—Jesse Jackson himself, the most visible leader of the 25-million-person black minority and possibly the most controversial man in America; the schools, those too-familiar local institutions that are still plagued by the same old problems despite many efforts to make changes; and the federal government, which of course shapes so much of American life. The mass media also played a minor role, as reporters' attempts to reflect the events objectively nevertheless had an influence on the events themselves. I will examine the actions of each of these actors in turn and then of course their interaction; for each of the players has ways of acting that are unknown, and perhaps unknowable, to the others. The dynamics of their interaction is what gave ultimate direction to the course of events that followed.

Ernest R. House

Acknowledgments

I would like to thank several people for the significant help they gave me in the writing and preparation of the manuscript. These include Eleanor Farrar, who worked on the government-funded case study of the PUSH/Excel evaluation with me; Sandra Mathison, who supplied several important ideas and suggestions to solve problems in the manuscript; and Colleen Frost and Carole Anderson, who typed and formatted the manuscript. Anthony Kraps, Steve Lapan, Pat Hays, Gene Glass, Noreen Michael, Royce Sadler, Gabe Della-Piana, Tom Hastings, Gordon Hoke, Clem Adelman, Saville Kushner, and Barry MacDonald all read various parts of the manuscript at different times and gave me useful feedback and encouragement. And a special thanks to Sally Furgeson of Westview Press, who took the manuscript in hand and made it happen; to Libby Barstow, who produced the book in record time; to Kathy Streckfus, for a beautiful final edit; and generally to Westview Press for an excellent job.

I would also like to thank those who worked on the original stakeholder evaluation project, including Bob Stake, Carol Weiss, David Cohen, Tony Bryk, and others in and around the University of Illinois, Harvard University, and the Huron Institute, all of whom were good intellectual company. I would also like to thank Norman Gold and his colleagues at the National Institute of Education for conscientiously and courageously funding the metaevaluation, although perhaps the results did not turn out as they may have hoped. Some of the data reported here were derived from that study. Both the government officials and the American Institutes for Research staffers were generous with their time and no doubt irritated with me for judging their evaluation to be misdirected, even while they acknowledged many of the deficiencies I pointed out. Although no one seems to have found workable solutions to these problems, at least there are people who keep trying.

E.R.H.

Introduction

The story of PUSH/Excel was derived from dozens of interviews with participants and observers as well as an examination of documents of various kinds, including media accounts, official memos and letters, and the American Institutes for Research (AIR) evaluation reports themselves.

Evaluations of major government social programs such as PUSH/Excel are standard practice. Ordinarily, research organizations compete for contracts to conduct evaluations by submitting proposals in response to government Requests for Proposals, which delineate the specific requirements of the evaluation desired. In this case, AIR won the contract to conduct the evaluation of PUSH/Excel. Their four technical evaluation reports will be discussed in detail in Chapters 6 and 7.

Critiques and studies of the evaluations themselves, however, are not common. In this case, federal officials hoped that they had discovered a way of conducting evaluations of highly political programs that would solve some of the problems such evaluations usually encountered. This approach to evaluation was employed initially with two highly political programs—Jackson's PUSH/Excel program and the Cities-in-Schools program, which was a favorite of Rosalynn Carter. To test this approach, the federal officials also contracted for a study of the evaluation itself as it was employed in these two cases. This second contract was won by the Huron Institute of Cambridge, Massachusetts, with our Center for Instructional Research and Curriculum Evaluation at the University of Illinois as a partner. This is the study that I refer to in this book as the case study of the evaluation, or the metaevaluation, and this is the point at which I became involved in studying the PUSH/Excel program. Our original report, "The Federalization of Jesse Jackson: The Story of PUSH/Excel's Evaluation," was completed in November 1982. It was later summarized in *New Directions for Program Evaluation* (Farrar and House 1983).

With Eleanor Farrar, my colleague on the case study project, I conducted interviews with more than forty people who were involved in PUSH/

Excel. We either tape-recorded the interviews, took notes, or both and summarized the interviews shortly thereafter. The persons, times, and places of the most important of those interviews have been cited in the References.

Even though the data for this book constitutes considerably more information than most accounts of activities surrounding Jesse Jackson, there are important gaps in the information. The major missing piece is a direct interview with Jackson himself, although I have tried repeatedly to obtain one, even to the point of sending him an earlier version of the manuscript for his comments. For reasons not clear to me, he chose to remain silent, other than what he had already said in the media. Perhaps he had had enough of social scientists, or perhaps he was trying to cut his losses, or perhaps he was simply too busy. I don't know.

I do have a letter from Mary Frances Berry, U.S. civil rights commissioner and former president of the PUSH/Excel board, saying that the portrayal of the PUSH/Excel program "does a remarkable job of describing what happened with PUSH/Excel." She did consent to be interviewed and also responded to an earlier version of the manuscript. And there were numerous interviews with all of the other PUSH/Excel principals—only Jackson is missing.

When citing interviews in the text, I have identified the main participants, such as PUSH/Excel and government officials, by name, as these specifics should be part of the program history. Those who played minor roles I have often identified only by position.

The AIR evaluation reports are actually quite thorough in describing the local program themselves. The on-site AIR observers did their jobs well by sending in extensive reports of local program activities and even reported on the politics surrounding some of the programs.

I did not, however, have access to the PUSH/Excel documents internal to the Chicago home office, nor does anyone else, so far as I know. Operation PUSH considers this information to be private. The same is true of the financial records, and what information I have about the internal budgeting problems comes from audits the federal government conducted when the handling of funds became an issue shortly after President Ronald Reagan took office.

I pulled all this information together in what I hoped would be a coherent and readable narrative that would reflect the many viewpoints of the participants. I looked for agreement between observations and observers. Where possible, I tried to include the word-for-word opinions of those who did not agree with my eventual interpretation of events. Certainly, other reasonable interpretations are possible. I also tried to include data and information that my own interpretation could not explain.

While doing research for the case study, I became fascinated by Jesse Jackson and by the larger turn of events as his attempt to reform the public schools and help black teenagers unfolded. I had previously conducted several studies of efforts to make changes in the schools; this one was similar in some ways and quite different in others. After we completed our contractual study for the government and published the results, I tried to make sense of the larger events I had witnessed and had heard about from others. This book is the product of that attempt.

It focuses on the interaction among Jesse Jackson, the public schools, the federal government, the mass media, and racial conflict in America. I must stress that although I think this is as balanced an account as one is likely to obtain of these events—an attempt at social science fairness and impartiality—it is not a totally flattering picture of the participants or institutions involved. Nor does it place the entire blame on any single factor. My analysis points to the complex underlying pattern of race relations in the United States as an ultimate explanation, which I shall elaborate in the latter half of the book. The book is divided into two basic parts—first the story of PUSH/Excel as it happened and then an explanation of why it occurred as it did.

1

The Most Controversial Man in America

All famous men and women have legends woven about them. Some they weave themselves, some their enemies weave, and some are simply exaggerations of characteristics they possess in modest degree writ larger by followers who have a need to cast the stories in particular ways. Thus we have George Washington's cherry tree and Abraham Lincoln's long walk to return a library book. Sometimes it takes decades or even centuries to sort the truth from the fiction. Often we never know for certain whether we have succeeded. These apocryphal stories are even stronger and more difficult to disentangle when the central person is controversial. One must be cautious in interpretation.

And no person in the 1980s has been more controversial than Jesse Jackson. He is revered, feared, and despised by vast numbers of people; few Americans are neutral about him. Partly this is because he has been the most visible leader of the 25-million-person black minority in the United States. Partly it is because of his leadership style. And perhaps it is partly because he himself contains many contradictions in his character, which make him fascinating, just as the United States is one of the most fascinating countries in the world because of its internal contradictions.

During the 1984 presidential campaign the *New York Times* summarized Jackson's public image this way:

Mr. Jackson is perceived by many as a man of energy with a probing mind, a silver tongue and a strong charisma, not just an ability to sway crowds but also personal charm and persuasiveness in one-on-one settings. And he is given credit for drawing attention to the needs of blacks, working to motivate school children and creating new business opportunities for black people.

But he is also seen as an egocentric power seeker who upstages other black leaders and pursues publicity for accomplishments that others achieve with less fanfare. And Operation PUSH, which he founded in Chicago 12 years ago, is seen as poorly administered; questions have been raised about its management of federal money (Joyce 1983).

This fascination with Jackson was more personally revealed in the words of two CBS reporters who followed him throughout his presidential campaign. They introduced their book about his 1984 campaign, *Thunder in America*, this way:

This book is an attempt by two reporters to come to terms with Jesse Louis Jackson. "Thunder," to the United States Secret Service detail which guarded him; "Reverend," to his staff; "one hundred and ninety pounds of intellectual dynamite . . . a bad black dude . . . our Savior," to adoring congregations. And a conniving, grandstanding Elmer Gantry to his detractors. We found him playing all those roles—and more (Faw and Skelton 1986, 1).

Many black Americans looked to Jackson as their national leader, the successor to Martin Luther King, Jr. In national polls Jackson was among the most admired public figures in America, respected by blacks and whites alike, one of the few blacks so honored. When the national media wanted to know what blacks thought about an issue, they invariably turned to Jackson for an opinion. He appeared at the side of presidents and celebrities. Yet at the same time—during the 1984 campaign—he received more threats on his life than all the other presidential candidates combined. The danger surrounding him was so tangible that photographers near him wore bullet-proof vests, and Geraldine Ferraro, the Democratic vice presidential candidate, told her children not to stand close to him in public for fear of violence (Faw and Skelton 1986).

It was significant that other prominent black leaders, among them Julian Bond and Mayor Andrew Young of Atlanta, also followers of Martin Luther King, expressed reservations about Jackson's bid for the presidency. There had been conflict between Jackson and the inner circle of King's Southern Christian Leadership Conference (SCLC) following King's assassination. Reverend Ralph Abernathy had introduced a book highly critical of Jackson with thinly veiled references: "What is needed today is not *charisma* so much as *character*. We had both in Martin Luther King, but we always knew that the character came first and was the most substantial part of the man. Now perhaps we will have to settle for a little bit less charisma and demand a little more character" (Abernathy 1985, vii). Why has Jackson been so controversial? I will trace some of the reported events that cast him in a controversial light, events leading to the story of PUSH/Excel. Later I will explore some of the deep-seated reasons for Jackson's image, with PUSH/Excel in the foreground.

Jackson's Early Career

Two biographies of Jackson exist, one by Barbara Reynolds, originally published in 1975 and reissued in 1985, and one by Eddie Stone, published in 1979. The one by Reynolds is substantial and authoritative, based on considerable first-hand interviewing. The tone of her book is critical, seemingly that of a woman who was enthralled with Jackson and what he stood for and then disenchanted. The one by Stone is comparatively slight and noncritical, more of an admiring campaign biography. Both biographies are fascinating reading. Their portrayals of his childhood point clearly to why he has such an intense personal need for leadership, recognition, and respect. Raised as an illegitimate child in a small town, he has always sought the respect he thought lacking, even in his younger years. Furthermore, the early events in Jackson's career indicate why he is so controversial. These issues will all be explored more fully in later chapters. For now, I caution against judging Jackson's controversial background at face value.

In 1965 Martin Luther King was facing difficulties in the demonstrations in Selma, Alabama. Violence had erupted, and he called upon everyone in the civil rights movement to come to Selma to help. Jackson, then a student at the Chicago Theological Seminary, organized half the students there and led them to Alabama. At the height of the demonstrations, King, Abernathy, and the top leaders of the Southern Christian Leadership Conference addressed the demonstrators from the steps of city hall. During a lull Jackson himself—totally unknown and uninvited—climbed the steps and addressed the crowd. The SCLC leaders were appalled at his audacity, but the crowd and media responded enthusiastically and King commended him personally.

Other SCLC leaders were unhappy about Jackson's impertinence. Andrew Young said, "I remember getting a little annoyed because Jesse was giving orders from the steps of Brown chapel and nobody knew who he was" (Reynolds 1975, 54). However, Ralph Abernathy was impressed with the young man, and when Jackson asked for a job, Abernathy convinced Martin Luther King to hire him. So Jackson was given a job organizing black ministers for the SCLC in Chicago.

The next year King decided to begin activities in Chicago to give SCLC a national platform instead of solely a southern base. The usual strategy was to organize through the local black ministers, who would bring their congregations into the effort. However, none of Chicago's ministers wanted to risk offending Mayor Richard Daley. Jackson took on the task of meeting with ministers one-on-one, and by the time King arrived, he had organized considerable support. Reportedly, King and his staff were met at O'Hare Airport by a limousine driven by Jackson himself. The next day, a mass rally was held at Soldier Field; King was impressed (Reynolds 1975, 65).

After failing to reach an agreement with Daley on open housing, King led demonstration marches into various sections of Chicago, such as Gage Park, Marquette Park, and Cragin, where the protesters encountered violently racist crowds. As SCLC leaders were contemplating what to do next, Jackson appeared on television and announced that they would march into Cicero, regarded as the most racist section of Chicago. That decision had not been made by the SCLC leadership, and Jackson had no authority for making such an announcement. A King staff member said, "The march announcement came one night when the cameras were on him. He couldn't resist saying something sensational that would get his name in the papers" (Reynolds 1975, 65).

Although the SCLC staff was again appalled, King decided to proceed with the march anyhow. Fearing racial violence, Mayor Daley capitulated and signed an open housing agreement, which proved to be worthless because the Chicago authorities never implemented it. King then organized a voter registration drive in Chicago in 1966 geared toward the 1967 mayoral election, but this effort also failed miserably. Daley had the city locked up through the apathy of black voters and the strength of his political machine.

> The movement had come up against America's most powerful local machine and had lost. The test case had been a failure, and Martin Luther King's Southern Christian Leadership Conference would never quite recover. They had played ball in the "minor" leagues of the South and had won their share of games. Once they stepped into the huge stadium of the Northern power-brokers, they found themselves leaving town with their tails between their legs (Stone 1979, 70).

There was one man, though, who thought he was ready to play in the major leagues. As the SCLC headed south, it left twenty-five-year-old Jesse Jackson in charge with only a small staff.

Jackson had been running the economic arm of SCLC, called Operation Breadbasket, and he thought that economics was the key to making changes in northern cities. "'We are the margin of profit of every major item produced in America from General Motors cars on down to Kellogg's Corn Flakes. If we've got his margin of profit, we've got his genitals,'

Jackson said" (Stone 1979, 74). He organized selective boycotts against white businesses modeled after those in Philadelphia led by the Reverend Leon Sullivan. The SCLC would target a particular business, then black ministers would convince their congregations to boycott that business until the company provided jobs for blacks. The first boycott, against Country Delight Dairy, secured 44 jobs; another, against High Low Foods, gained 184. Red Rooster, a firm allegedly selling putrid food to blacks, eventually went out of business because of the boycotts. Jackson also persuaded black merchants to deposit money in banks owned by blacks, and the deposits in these banks quickly increased fourfold. The banks could then lend the money to black businesses. This strategy was a major reason for Jackson's influence (Reynolds 1975, 177).

King's Assassination

In 1968, King and his staff gathered in Memphis to support the striking sanitation workers. At 6 P.M. on April 4, just outside his motel room, King was shot in the head by an assassin. Ralph Abernathy, his longtime friend, rushed to his side and cradled the dying man's head in his arms. Someone brought a towel to press against King's wound in a vain attempt to stop the bleeding.

An ambulance came and King was taken to St. Joseph's Hospital. The first television camera crews arrived at 6:25 P.M., and it was agreed among King's aides that no one would talk to the media. When Hosea Williams looked out the window of his motel room, however, he saw Jesse Jackson talking to the television reporters. When Williams went outside, he heard Jackson say, "Yes, I was the last man in the world King spoke to" (Reynolds 1975, 89). Williams was infuriated because Jackson had not even been physically close to King when he was shot. Williams tried to climb over the railing to "stomp him into the ground" but was restrained by a policeman. Later that night ABC News reported that Jackson had been by King's side when he was shot, and this story was repeated in the media.

That night Ralph Abernathy, the heir apparent to King, gave Jackson permission to return to Chicago to organize mourners to come to the funeral. The rest of the staff remained in Memphis, still not speaking to the press. At 6 A.M. the next morning, twelve hours after King had been shot, they were astounded to see Jesse Jackson on the NBC "Today Show." He was wearing the same turtleneck shirt he had worn the night before, only now it was stained with blood, which he claimed was Martin Luther King's. Jackson also appeared in the same shirt later that day to berate the Chicago City Council. The staffers were furious. Clearly, Jackson was making a bid to replace King, and the blood on his shirt, if it was King's, could only have come from the towel placed on King's wound. According to eyewitnesses, Jackson had not been near King when he was shot.

That Saturday at the Operation Breadbasket memorial services, 4,000 people attended compared to 400 the week before. As Jackson stood on the stage, behind him was a huge photo of King with another photo of Jackson beneath, as if the mantle of leadership was passing from King to Jackson. Jackson addressed the crowd as the new leader of the black people; even the cadence of his speech resembled King's. In the weeks following the assassination, Jackson moved deliberately to replace King as the premier black leader. He met with his public relations people, and they designed a media strategy to project Jackson as the successor. In November 1969 *Playboy* magazine proclaimed Jackson "King's heir apparent," and in an introduction to an interview with Jackson, *Playboy* repeated the story of King dying in Jackson's arms. In April 1970 *Time* magazine featured Jackson in a cover story, and he appeared on numerous talk shows, where he was always impressive.

For their part the SCLC staff felt that Jackson was a cold-blooded opportunist who would do anything to gain publicity and seize power (Stone 1979, 149). While they were lamenting King's death, Jackson was already taking over, furthering his own interests and usurping the role that SCLC staff members thought rightfully belonged to Ralph Abernathy. They called Jackson a "hot dog" and a media hound, and a split developed between the SCLC and Jackson that would never quite be healed.

In any case, within a short time following King's assassination, Jackson was a national figure. He had devised a strategy to secure national leadership, and the media played a critical role in helping him achieve his goal. From the time of Booker T. Washington through Martin Luther King, the press had traditionally accepted only one primary black spokesman at the time. What did blacks think about this or that? The media always turned to one person who presumably represented the black viewpoint, and after King's death they chose Jackson for the black spokesman role. Jackson was highly articulate and photogenic. He was nonviolent yet said controversial things. He was not a reverse racist, he understood negotiation and compromise, and he struck deals businesses could tolerate. He was a capitalist and a preacher who had moral authority. He was trendy in dress and appeared with celebrities. Thomas Todd, one of Jackson's former colleagues from Operation PUSH, once said, "Jesse understands the media well and has learned to use it well. He combines everything the media wants. He looks good, he sounds good and he excites passion, good and bad" (Joyce 1983).

In assessing the events following King's assassination, one of Jackson's biographers was more sympathetic than the SCLC staffers. Stone said that Jackson "seized a tragic moment in history and took hold of the reins . . . " (1979, 29). According to this view, blacks needed a new national leader and the whites needed them to have one. Jackson was ready. "His attitudes were always aggressive, his style always play to win" (Stone 1979, 39).

The Struggle over Leadership

Having gained national prominence, from 1968 to 1971 Jackson dueled with Ralph Abernathy for the black leadership. While running Operation Breadbasket in Chicago, Jackson not only employed the selective boycott but introduced new strategies of his own design. As a result, products from black-owned businesses began appearing on store shelves, and he encouraged blacks to buy these products. "You will show your blackness by buying Grove Fresh orange juice. Say it loud. I'm black and I'm proud and I buy Grove Fresh orange juice" (Reynolds 1975, 163.) Or "Now, Joe Louis Milk does not come from a Negro cow. That milk has 400 USP like any other milk. Only difference is that your husband can make twelve thousand a year driving a truck for this company" (Drotning and South 1970, 37). Almost without exception, black businesses supported by Operation Breadbasket increased their sales, and blacks doing business with blacks produced many new black millionaires; those businesspeople contributed to Jackson's operation.

Jackson saw black economic power as an alternative to black violence, which he deplored. In his view, black capitalism was beneficial as long as it did not become too much like white capitalism—compassionate toward machines rather than people. The selective boycotts worked best with corporations in the ghetto, and selective patronage for black firms was bound to race. But poverty had no color, and Jackson talked about forming a "rainbow coalition."

Increasingly, Jackson turned toward direct involvement in politics, although here he was not so successful. In 1969 he led poor people's marches to Springfield, and in 1970 he began another series of battles with Mayor Daley, most of which he lost. Like others before him, he found Daley to be a wily opponent. In 1971 he launched an abortive and ill-conceived run for mayor of Chicago; he tried to establish a third political party, the Liberation party, without much success. In 1972 he helped set up a black political convention to endorse a presidential candidate but the meeting ended in disharmony. Jackson's political campaign was thwarted by the Black Congressional Caucus, which claimed to represent the black constituency, and by the entry of Shirley

Chisholm into the Democratic presidential race—someone for once upstaging Jesse Jackson. All in all, he found it difficult to convert civil rights activism and media coverage into votes. Blacks either did not vote or voted for machine candidates.

One of his most successful enterprises, again an economic venture, resulted in a final split with the SCLC. In 1968 Jackson initiated a Black Christmas, complete with a black Santa Claus, aimed at persuading blacks to do their Christmas shopping at black-owned stores. This tactic was highly effective and was followed by a Black Easter, and these events were combined into Black Expo in 1970, a massive celebration of blackness featuring black celebrities and products. Black Expo was hugely successful, by far the largest event of its type. Hundreds of thousands of people attended and paid entrance fees, and hundreds of firms, owned by blacks as well as whites, paid for the opportunity to exhibit. The event was held under the auspices of Operation Breadbasket and the SCLC.

At Black Expo 70, all signs of Ralph Abernathy were expunged from the Expo exhibits. Pictures featuring prominent black leaders included Jackson but omitted Abernathy, the official head of SCLC. The *Playboy* article proclaiming Jackson as King's heir apparent was distributed. The next year, at Expo 71, all associations with SCLC were severed, for Jackson had secretly incorporated Black Expo under its own charter. When Abernathy found out, he was furious and ordered an investigation into Black Expo finances. The financial accounting of Black Expo was inadequate: There was a discrepancy between the number of people attending and gross gate receipts reported. Although Jackson claimed ignorance of financial matters, he was called before the SCLC, chastised, and suspended from his position for a few months for breaking SCLC rules and procedures (Reynolds 1975, 325–356). He was furious. In December 1971 he resigned from SCLC and founded his own organization, Operation PUSH. Actually, the split had been developing from the day of King's assassination.

Operation PUSH

On Christmas Day, 1971, Jackson held a ceremony to celebrate the founding of PUSH (People United to Save Humanity, later changed to the more modest People United to Serve Humanity). He brought his staff and most of the Operation Breadbasket staff with him into the new organization. Prominent black businesspeople had been telling him for some time that they would support him no matter what the name of his organization, and the list of newly established PUSH board names read like a Black Who's Who. Mayor Richard Hatcher, Aretha Franklin,

Jim Brown, Ossie Davis, and celebrities like Hugh Hefner rushed to his assistance. By 1975 PUSH had about thirty chapters in different cities.

Operation PUSH was to be a "civil economics" organization, the goal of which was to secure jobs, organize those not making a livable wage, and support the growth of black-owned businesses. The selective boycotts now focused on the largest national corporations, and Jackson started signing "covenants" with corporations like Coca-Cola, Seven-Up, Burger King, and Heublein. These voluntary agreements committed the companies to hiring more blacks, doing business with minorities, awarding franchises and distributorships to blacks, making deposits in black-owned banks, advertising in black-owned publications, and donating money to black colleges and other organizations. One executive from Coors Brewery, a covenant partner, said that Jackson had the economic power to do harm to any major corporation (*Chicago Tribune* 1983a).

PUSH was also intended as a political organization, and in 1972 Jackson finally scored a major triumph over Mayor Daley by helping to unseat Daley's delegation to the Democratic National Convention. For the most part, however, veteran political observers thought that Jackson was not an effective force on the local political scene. Black voters did not register or else voted for the Daley machine. One Chicago politician said that Jackson's Saturday morning forum broadcast over the radio was his chief contribution to Chicago politics (Reynolds 1975, 218). But much of his effort focused nationally rather than locally.

Organizationally, PUSH appeared to be a one-man decision-making operation in which Jackson made all the decisions, and the others followed him as a band of disciples following the inspired directives of their leader. Often there was no systematic follow-through or attention to continuity in PUSH activities (Reynolds 1975, 288). Some said PUSH was more a movement than an organization, that the charismatic leader jumped from one issue to the next, depending on his intuitions. Departments and divisions within the organization were structured according to Jackson's current interests, and internal units dwindled as his interest waned. Issues also came and went. Depending upon national events, Jackson would address one issue one day and a different one a few weeks later. He used this method partly because he saw the purposes of the PUSH organization as a broad effort dedicated to addressing any problem that might arise for poor blacks, and the poor were cursed with any number of acute problems. Commenting on his own peripatetic behavior, Jackson said, "You can call me a gadfly if you wish. The job of a doctor is to show up where sick people are" (Reynolds 1975, 286). But because of this style, PUSH often did not complete one mission before proceeding to the next.

This roving quality was also caused by the necessity of keeping up with the media, of capturing the attention of the public. Jackson's major strategy for dealing with a problem was to focus the media upon it, to draw attention to the problem. In a sense, he was an "issue jockey," always creating or anticipating issues the media might respond to, and perhaps this style also satisfied his own need for recognition. The media were his lifeblood; the organization had to follow.

Another problem was his reluctance to delegate authority within the organization. His seconds-in-command never lasted long, and many former staffers related stories of how Jackson would set one staffer against another, perhaps in order to assure that no other person acquired too much power (Reynolds 1975, 289). If a staffer made a decision while Jackson was traveling, Jackson might come back and countermand it. Because he had the only real authority, staffers at all levels turned to him personally when they needed something done. Although PUSH staffers were highly dedicated, many felt stultified in the one-man structure and resigned after only a short time. Biographer Reynolds commented, "The PUSH platform is a national showcase for black excellence, with Jackson, the autocratic father figure, supplying the definitions of black man, black heroes, black anti-heros, black everything" (Reynolds 1975, 11).

Reynolds thought that much of the organization of Operation PUSH emulated the autocratic leadership of the Baptist church, historically the strongest institution in the black social order. Black ministers ruled their churches, and Jackson was the most famous preacher of them all. Traditionally, the black minister had the most respect of anyone in the black community, and black congregations were accustomed to following the leader without question. It was primarily black ministers who led the civil rights movement. Similarly, Jackson ruled PUSH in an autocratic and charismatic manner. He said, "I am anointed, not appointed" (Reynolds 1975, 292). There was no voting on important matters: The Reverend, as his staff called him, decided.

Nor was there any conventional accountability, except in the general sense that Jackson had to retain his following. This lack of accountability carried over into financial matters, and PUSH encountered legal difficulties several times, usually because of careless bookkeeping. Finances were kept entirely secret; they simply were not anybody else's business, in the view of PUSH leaders. Neither were criticism and dissent welcomed inside this autocratic structure. Critics were soundly denounced, and Jackson used his influence to curtail reporters who were critical of his work, just as many politicians do. One reporter, a regular member of the Saturday rallies, was publicly chastised in front of the entire congregation for revealing negative information. Operation PUSH, in fact, had much of the structure of a black Baptist church.

The Country Preacher

Jackson called himself "The Country Preacher," and an important source of his influence was the Saturday morning rally of Operation PUSH. Although he traveled as many as 200,000 miles each year, no matter where he was he would always return to Chicago for the Saturday morning service, held from 9 to 12 A.M. on Saturdays so as not to be in competition with other ministers for Sunday services. The 100-voice PUSH choir sang jazzed-up old-time hymns, bringing the audience to its feet in a frenzy of applause, dancing, and swaying to the rhythm. Jackson would lead the congregation in his famous chant:

I am—Somebody!
I may be poor, but I am—Somebody!
I may be on welfare, but I am—Somebody!
I may be uneducated, but I am—Somebody!
I may be in jail, but I am—Somebody!
I am—Somebody!

Sometimes Jackson would be dressed in a dashiki, in bell-bottom trousers and turtleneck, or in expensive jeans. Around his neck he wore a gold-plated medallion commemorating Martin Luther King. In his speech he used the chant, the cadences, and the question-response pattern of the tent preachers, the revivalists. Behind him were large photographs of himself and King, reminding his audience that he was King's heir. Dramatic lighting and visuals underscored his splendid rhetoric. The service was emotionally charged, and Jackson used his voice like a musical instrument. Reynolds described Jackson on the podium: "As Jackson leans forward on the podium, it is little wonder that the audience worships this man. Sensuous in black leather vest, striped T-shirt, and tight leather pants; 220 pounds of muscle rippling through a six-foot two-inch frame; billowing Afro; a sculpted face; the Country Preacher projects all the manly qualities that most blacks respect" (Reynolds 1975, 8).

The service was carried over the radio to local and national audiences, and the familiar chants and the powerful preaching created a vast constituency for Jackson, by many accounts the greatest preacher since King and superior to King in his use of the media. His Saturday morning services, his rallies, and his public actions were carefully staged. "'I'm a preacher,' Jackson said, 'but primarily I'm an organizer and a programmer. In a sense the civil rights movement is a drama, but you have to keep setting the stage and creating scenes that people can act their way out of if they are to make maximum progress'" (Drotning and South 1970, 21).

Jackson staged political rallies as well as religious ones. In 1969, in support of sustaining welfare payments in Illinois Governor Richard Ogilvie's budget, Jackson packed the galleries of the Illinois General Assembly with his supporters. The legislator who had introduced the bill to cut welfare payments withdrew his proposed cuts after a stirring speech by Jackson, which was cheered by the packed galleries and covered by the media. Actually, the agreement to withdraw the cuts had been made the day before as a political favor in return for Jackson's support of Ogilvie, a Republican, for governor (Reynolds 1975, 194). The appeal to the General Assembly was an enactment after the fact, but it was highly successful in demonstrating Jackson's concern for the poor and the effectiveness of his campaign. In these symbolic actions, Jackson excelled.

So by 1975 at the age of thirty-four, Jackson was, if not the most powerful black leader in America, certainly the most visible. He possessed tremendous charisma in the black community. Sometimes he was referred to as the Black Jesus, the Black Messiah, or the Black Moses, and he made effective use of his religious status in establishing and maintaining his charisma. In his rise to national power he was strongly supported by segments of the popular media, with cover stories in *Playboy, Time, Penthouse,* the *New York Times,* and many others. He was featured almost weekly in *Jet.* By 1973 he had appeared on 1,515 talk shows. Some said that he never missed an opportunity to appear on television, and his charm and mastery of different dialects served him well. He always had something controversial to say, which made for good television, and he could look militant and evoke fierce racial pride. At the same time he preached nonviolence and was able to negotiate with the white power structure. Even ultraconservative Phyllis Schlafly could support Jackson's position that racial integration through busing was not necessarily the only answer (Reynolds 1975, 373).

Biographer Stone thought that some of Jackson's appeal derived from the appearance of constant motion, the appearance of always doing something. Jackson moved in and out of cities quickly, dramatically, and with flair. His massive rallies and demonstrations fueled his charisma, and television viewers were treated to spectacles of adoring followers. Jackson filled the public's appetite for movement, action, and glamour, and like the president he was always flying off somewhere to be greeted by large audiences and important people. Jackson's private life reinforced his public image. He socialized with such entertainment personalities as Jim Brown, Roberta Flack, Nancy Wilson, and Hugh Hefner. Later, he was at President Jimmy Carter's side as the most visible black leader of the time. Stone said he was perceived as:

> a high-flyer, a swinger who jets back and forth across the country, mingles with the beautiful people and is continually fighting off beautiful women. Jackson does nothing to dispel that image. He dresses sharply and expensively, wearing custom-made buckskin and leather jackets, Italian boots and silk shirts. When he walks onto a stage, everyone in the house knows that he is one black cat who has made it (Stone 1979, 163).

According to Stone, it was the credibility of this image that enabled Jackson to deliver his work-hard, study-hard Calvinistic message to black teenagers. No one would have listened to a colorless Ralph Abernathy. Meanwhile, Jackson lived in a fifteen-room mansion with his five children and wife, Jackie, whom he had married in 1962. He did not smoke or drink, had a chauffeur-driven limousine, and wore expensive clothes, and he saw no reason why he should not enjoy the good things in life while he was helping others to obtain them.

His major critics within the black community faulted him for using his influence, power, and position to further his own interests at the expense of poor blacks. They thought that Jackson had gotten too close to wealthy businesspeople and the white establishment, that he was leading a "silver rights" rather than a civil rights movement, and that he had used his power to build a personal patronage system. But among blacks he had a huge devoted following. In the face of this criticism, Jackson remained unperturbed, his confidence unshaken. Harkening back to his childhood, Jackson said, "Public ridicule will either crush you or challenge you; it can take away your spirit or stimulate your adrenaline. I chose the achievement route." Jackson's longtime friend Robert Tucker said, "Jesse not only believes in God, but he firmly believes God believes in him" (Joyce 1983). When he made mistakes he referred to himself as an "imperfect tool" or a "frail vessel" and bounced back with amazing resilience.

In 1975 Jesse Jackson turned his considerable talents, influence, and sense of mission to educational reform. He would create an educational program that would help black teenagers in the big cities, whom he saw as too often self-destructive and "out of control." His creation, PUSH for Excellence, was destined to be as spectacular and as controversial as its creator.

PART ONE

Jesse Jackson and the PUSH/Excel Program

2

A Great Idea

On December 4, 1977, Jackson was interviewed by reporter Dan Rather on the television program "60 Minutes." Jackson said:

Now the challenge is upward mobility, and that is why the focus on not only getting in school, but producing in school, becomes a new kind of challenge. In other words, we can get into the new school by law, but to become a doctor, lawyer, engineer will require intense effort. We must struggle to excel because competition is keener, because doors that once opened are now closing in our faces. It's my judgment we need a massive revolution in our attitude.

But we cannot do it alone. We must be a catalyst. That's a role. But then many other people must get involved. I'm not trying to do it alone. We pulled together a group of ministers, churches around each school, because many parents will not fit into the PTA structure. But if the minister, in fact, will share the PTA agenda with his congregants, then that is a way of having massive parent involvement. We've begun to mobilize disc jockeys and key athletes and artists and entertainers who make [an] impact upon children's minds. So in a real sense, what we're doing is not operating alone; we're simply using our talent and energy to mobilize involvement to take on a massive problem.

Hubert Humphrey was watching "60 Minutes" from his hospital bed in Minneapolis when he heard Jackson speak of the need for a movement to convince black youths to excel in school. The program showed Jackson's impassioned appeal to a stadium full of wildly applauding teenagers in Los Angeles and his call to the black community to come forward and participate in the endeavor. The next day Humphrey called his old friend, Joseph Califano, secretary of the Department of Health, Education, and Welfare (HEW).

In a weak voice, his strength consumed by his battle with cancer, [Humphrey] asked me if I had seen the "60 Minutes" program. When I responded, he

21

said, 'Well, then you saw what I saw. I want you to talk to Jesse Jackson
and help him. He's doing something for those kids. I've talked to him this
morning and told him I'll talk to you. Now you get him down to your office
and help him. Will you do that for me?" I told him I would (Califano 1981,
294).

Within a few days Califano called Jackson to his office. Jackson and
his director of operations, Dr. Charles Warfield, had prepared a letter
outlining the needs of the program and requesting about $25,000 in
federal aid. Califano took the lead in the discussion, and as he talked,
Jackson and Warfield realized that Califano was talking about millions
of dollars in federal assistance rather than a few thousand. Speaking in
an interview in 1980, Warfield said he had quietly crumpled their modest
request in his hand as Califano talked on.

Dr. Mary Frances Berry, then assistant secretary of HEW for Education
and later president of the PUSH/Excel Board and U.S. civil rights
commissioner, recalled in an interview in 1982 that after Califano's
conversation with Humphrey, Secretary Califano called Jackson to Washington to offer funding for PUSH/Excel but Jackson refused the money,
saying that the program was not yet fully developed. Califano then
enlisted Berry's help to convince Jackson to accept federal support. He
told Jackson that it wasn't important that he had no developed program;
Jackson could hire a writer to prepare a funding proposal and the
government would provide assistance. Whether there was actually a
program would become a critical issue later, during the federally sponsored
evaluation of PUSH/Excel. In any event, however reluctantly, Jackson
accepted the offer of federal assistance with the notion that the money
could be used for program development.

Thus began the federal government's involvement in PUSH/Excel, a
motivational program for black youth started by Jackson two years earlier
and until then supported by private contributions. One month later, the
National Institute of Education (NIE), a HEW agency, awarded two
grants to the PUSH Foundation: $25,000 to plan a conference and
$20,000 for evaluation and project design. Five months later, NIE awarded
another $400,000 to support projects in Chicago, Kansas City, and Los
Angeles and prepared to expand to additional sites. Next, the U.S. Office
of Education, also part of HEW, began planning for a $3 million
demonstration project to begin in January 1979. By May 1978, more
than twenty local education agencies had expressed interest in becoming
part of the demonstration (S. Murray et al. 1982, 24).

Not everyone shared Humphrey's enthusiasm for a federal role in
PUSH/Excel. A few days after his conversation with Humphrey, Califano
called Patricia Graham, then director of the National Institute of Education

and later dean of the Harvard School of Education. Graham reported that:

> [Califano said] there was this great thing called Excel. "Got any money?" I said, "No money for operating programs. Planning, evaluation. But no operating money." I called around the country to a variety of people and said, "What about Jesse Jackson, and should we put money into his operation?" It seems to me that the basic question is, can you bottle charisma, and organize it? And people said, "Well, yes." And they said, he's also had trouble keeping his books straight. . . .
>
> [Then Jackson came to see me and I said] "There's money for you to plan a proposal . . . which we will evaluate. Obviously you don't have to do that, but if you take federal cash, then you have to be able to account for how the cash is spent, and you have to specify what it is you're going to do with that cash. And the gist of the evaluation is whether or not you did what you said you were going to do. So the crux of it is figuring out what it is that you're going to do and how you're going to do it." . . . This was shortened, of course. It was about an eight-month discussion (Graham 1981).

So the form federal involvement would take was this: The National Institute of Education would provide money for planning and be in charge of the evaluation (evaluation was required for most federal educational projects, and PUSH/Excel was no exception), and the Office of Education would provide money for program operation, development, and demonstration. The latter components would require most of the money, which would go to the national PUSH/Excel office in Chicago and to the cooperating cities for the demonstration sites.

The whole federal enterprise was initiated from the top down, from Califano's office, through Mary Frances Berry as assistant secretary. Bureaucrats at lower levels were not involved in the initial decision. Berry's style of operation was to issue orders and expect those orders to be obeyed. She gave orders to her staff to support PUSH/Excel and delegated the responsibility for the details to those under her. "It seemed to all of us it was a great idea," she said. "We thought everyone else would think it was a good idea" (Berry 1982b). But the bureaucrats at the lower levels had their own ideas as to what worked and what to fund, and from Berry's later perspective, they were uncooperative. In retrospect, she wished that she had assigned one of her staff members full-time to "honcho" the decision all the way through, to monitor the operation. But she did not do so, and she later blamed the actions of the federal government for the difficulties that ensued, claiming that the government did not follow through on its promises to Jackson. The PUSH/Excel idea itself was sound, she thought; but others in the government blamed Jackson and PUSH/Excel (Berry 1982b).

The Origins of PUSH/Excel

The development of PUSH/Excel as a program was not simple or straightforward. For one thing, Excel had been launched as a movement—a grass-roots, self-help effort to achieve a broad set of goals through personal and community commitment. It was not a structured educational reform with a blueprint for implementation. Furthermore, the people who staffed the national office were people who knew how to work with broad-based movements, not educators or program developers. Their experience came from the civil rights movement, and they knew more about strategies to promote such movements than about negotiating the intricacies of large school districts. The PUSH/Excel national staff lacked technocratic skills as well as bureaucratic experience. Another complication was that the Excel staff expected local sites to develop their own programs, which was not an easy task. So at the time that federal involvement began, what existed was an eloquent, charismatic leader of national reputation who had attracted a staff of committed followers, considerable public and private funding, and several school districts willing to attempt the translation of his self-help philosophy into a school program to regenerate black youth. According to the official history of PUSH/Excel, the program grew out of the protest staged by Operation PUSH at the White House on January 15, 1975, to demonstrate for a full employment economy and jobs for blacks. The demonstration began as planned but was ended abruptly when Jackson told the marchers to go home. A letter from the PUSH/Excel Board of Directors to potential donors explained Jackson's decision:

> Walking through file after file of protesters, a tall, athletic, young black minister—a man who had been in the vanguard of the civil rights movement for years—was shocked to see that a great many of the youths were drunk or on drugs, visibly out of control.
>
> That man, the Reverend Jesse Jackson, realized then that the time had come for him to change his target for reform. As he painfully said: "The door of opportunity is open for our people, but they are too drunk, too unconscious to walk through the door" (*PUSH for Excellence*, n.d.).

Ten months later Jackson appeared before a student assembly at Chicago's predominantly black Martin Luther King High School, and his message was that it was up to blacks to make sure they did not waste what opportunities they had. As Jackson put it, "No one will save us for us but us." It was the first stop in a cross-country tour that the *Washington Post* described as "Jesse Jackson's Crusade" (S. Murray et al. 1982, 12).

The Message of the Crusade

˙Jackson's crusade stressed the message that hard work, self-discipline, delayed gratification, and persistence were the qualities youth needed in order to succeed. He felt that this familiar Calvinist refrain needed to be revived because black youths blamed society for their failures and expected it to provide redress. "Even as we argue this victim-victimizer argument, it is very clear in my mind that we are the victims and the oppressor is the victimizer. Now having said that, the oppressor is not going to run the race and give you his or her gold medal" (Jackson 1977, 189).

The civil rights movement had convinced blacks that they were not to blame for their misfortune, but Jackson felt that it had also convinced many of them that "the system" was now responsible for providing easy access to the rewards it had previously denied them. He hoped to replace this futile aspiration with one based on sacrifice and commitment to personal goals. In a speech in Los Angeles Jackson said:

> There's one thing worse than not having an opportunity—that's having one and not taking advantage of it. There's one thing worse than being in a slum—that's to mess around and let a slum get in you. . . . You cannot be what you ought to be if you are pickling your brains with liquor and using easy access to guns to destroy each other. You cannot be what you ought to be if you put dope in your veins instead of hope in your brain (Jesse Jackson speech in Los Angeles, July 1977, quoted in S. Murray et al. 1982).

The main target of Jackson's message was black teenagers, and he believed that the resources of the entire community had to be mobilized to help, including parents, churches, schools, and businesses. He urged parents to take an interest in their children's schooling, to establish regular study hours at home, and to pick up report cards at school. Teachers were admonished to set higher standards for behavior and academic performance and to see to it that students attained them and were rewarded. Churches, businesses, and community members were urged to lend their support, to reinforce the self-help ethic by participating in events, contributing time and money, and recognizing successful students with awards and opportunities.

In brief, Jackson encouraged black youth to strive toward solid, middle-class virtues, and tried to rally the total involvement of the students and their communities. He advocated a tripod of student support, with the parents on one side, the schools on another, and the community, especially the churches, on the third leg. Assigning the church such a prominent role reflected Jackson's own southern background and the origins of his movement. He elaborated his approach in what he initially called The Ten Commandments, and later more modestly renamed The Ten Principles:

1. It is essential that a public institution clearly define itself, to say unequivocally what it believes in and stands for.
2. The development of responsible adults is a task requiring community commitment. It cannot be left solely to the public schools.
3. The principal tasks of the public schools cannot be achieved if a disproportionate amount of time and resources must be given to maintaining order. Public schools are not obligated to serve students who persistently disrupt schools and violate the rights of others.
4. The full responsibility for learning cannot be transferred from the student to the teacher.
5. Parents must consistently support the proposition that students have responsibilities as well as rights and that the schools have an obligation to insist upon both.
6. High performance takes place in a framework of expectation.
7. There is nothing inherently undemocratic in requiring students to do things that are demonstrably beneficial to them.
8. Involvement in and commitment to meaningful activities which give one a sense of identity and worth are essential to all human beings and are especially critical to adolescents.
9. The practice of convenience leads to collapse, but the laws of sacrifice lead to greatness. This applies to students, teachers, parents, administrators, and community leaders.
10. A sound *ethical* climate must be established for a school system as a whole and for each individual school, because the death of ethics is the sabotage of excellence. Politicians, school board members, superintendents, central office staff, principals, teachers, parents, and ministers have the obligation to take an aggressive lead in setting such ethical standards (*PUSH for Excellence: The Developing Process of Implementation*, n.d., 4–5).

Momentum Builds

At first, PUSH/Excel was more a message than a program, and a strongly Calvinist message at that, but the media supported Jackson's crusading efforts. In 1975 and 1976 the *Chicago Sun-Times* and the *Washington Post* ran several articles about PUSH/Excel and syndicated columnist William Raspberry wrote a series of columns lauding the effort. From 1975 to 1978 the program gained great momentum, primarily because of Jackson's efforts as reported in the media. His message of self-help and high standards of achievement struck responsive chords wherever he went, which seemed to be everywhere. In the cities where he spoke, audiences filled the stadiums, television and newspapers recorded his successes, editorials praised the wisdom of his self-help pronouncements, and nationally televised talk shows invited him to appear.

In spring 1976 the Chicago Board of Education consented to initiate the program in ten schools, and activities were begun in September. In 1977 planning was begun in Kansas City and Los Angeles, at the request of local groups in those cities, and dozens of other school districts made inquiries (S. Murray et al. 1982). These early activities were mostly underwritten by corporate and philanthropic contributors; Excel received $260,000 from various contributors in 1977. Local school districts also began allocating some of their own funds for local Excel programs: Los Angeles set aside $403,000 for the program in ten schools (S. Murray and C. Murray 1980). In that year alone Jackson made more than forty appearances across the country and on television on behalf of PUSH/Excel, and it was in December that he appeared on "60 Minutes" to set the stage for federal involvement.

The following year, 1978, PUSH/Excel was endorsed by the Louisiana governor and the superintendent of schools, with the Louisiana legislature setting aside $300,000 for a New Orleans project. In May a conference was held at Howard University, and many prominent black educators heard and endorsed Jackson's ideas. By this time federal money had begun arriving. In addition to the total of $445,000 in grants from the NIE, in 1979 PUSH/Excel received $700,000 from the Office of Education and $500,000 from the Department of Labor. Chicago, Los Angeles, Kansas City, Denver, and Chattanooga were chosen as the major demonstration sites. In February $725,000 was allocated for the evaluation of PUSH/Excel, although that money went to the American Institutes for Research (AIR), the private contractor for the evaluation, not to PUSH/Excel. In March a PUSH/Excel rally in the New Orleans' Superdome drew more than 65,000 people, and in April in Los Angeles, 20,000 spectators watched Jackson, Marlon Brando, and Aretha Franklin in Dodger Stadium. *Denver Post* education editor Art Branscombe described the Denver rally held September 12, 1979, in an article entitled, "Sermon by Jackson Opens PUSH/Excel":

> The slim, dynamic Chicago Baptist minister . . . treated the students gathered on the Manual High School athletic field to one of his inimitable education revival sermons.
>
> Jackson, 38, told the multiracial throng that . . . "THE LORD MAKES oranges grow on trees, but you've got to squeeze the juice yourselves."
>
> "If you don't have much opportunity, but have a lot of will and desire, you'll make a way out of no way," he assured his cheering audience. "Your effort and desire must exceed your opportunity" (Branscombe 1979).

The Problems of Organizing in Operation PUSH

If the crusade became a sensation overnight, efforts to translate the initial message into a well-developed program proceeded slowly. The organizational base for the crusade was Operation PUSH, which was given the task of running the fund-raising and promotional activities while local staff developed and managed local operations. This structure fit the traditional decentralized organization of the civil rights movement, but it quickly became apparent that more central direction was necessary. Most local staff were inexperienced at community organizing and dealing with top-level school bureaucrats. The local staffs expected help from a national staff, which PUSH finally established in the spring of 1977 and housed in PUSH headquarters.

A PUSH/Excel national director and administrative aide were hired to design the program, coordinate local project activities, develop a structured approach, and expand the resource base. Almost from the beginning, however, the staff was occupied with the public relations task of helping Jackson spread the message. As interest in PUSH/Excel escalated, the national staff spent more time on the road with Jackson and responding to information requests than in developing the implementation tools that local staff members felt they needed.

Nor was working with Jackson conducive to developing teaching materials or lesson plans. At two or three in the morning staffers were likely to be awakened from their sleep by a phone call. "This is Jesse. Have you thought about. . . . " Or "This is Jesse. Pack your bag and meet me at the airport. We're going on the road." They might be gone for a month, with no hint of where they would be (Warfield 1980). Jackson burned out his staff quickly. His style of operation derived from his desire to be active, to always be doing something. This desire, in part, came from his association with Martin Luther King—Jackson felt that his own chances of a long life were slim. He instructed his aides, "Watch my back in a crowd. They'll get me one day but there's no use giving them a cheap shot" (Warfield 1980). His unusual work hours and busy schedule may have been intended to make his own actions unpredictable to potential assassins, and his concerns for his physical safety were not without foundation.

Despite these organizational problems and personal worries, by 1979 at least twenty-two independent programs had developed in cities across the country and looked to the national office for guidance. PUSH/Excel had become a national phenomenon.

3

The Program: Commitment and Self-Discipline

From the beginning, PUSH/Excel was a moral campaign. Jackson's introductory letter in the first PUSH/Excel document captured the tone precisely.

> As I talk with young people these days, I'm convinced that they are crying out for moral leadership and discipline. Their cry is evident in the schools. It's evident on the streets. Most disturbingly, it's evident in the home. The moral vacuum in which our children are living and growing up breeds an environment of disorder that makes it difficult, perhaps impossible, for many of them to define and achieve excellence in their lives.
>
> They need, and we need to provide for them, *a total refocusing of efforts away from non-productive distractions and other elements of temptation and toward those disciplines that will permit them to reach for and obtain the steep goal of excellence.* This refocusing of efforts, this PUSH for Excellence— especially academic excellence—calls for greater commitment from teachers, greater involvement from parents and greater discipline and harder work from students (*PUSH for Excellence*, n.d., 2).

Jackson saw a moral vacuum in society and in the home, not only for blacks but for whites as well. His solution was to move away from material temptations and instead move toward self-discipline. Salvation lay in personal commitment, commitment by the student, the parent, the teacher, and the community. The visible symbol of such commitment was the pledge—a public pledge by each person to strive for excellence. The three pledges for students, parents, and teachers went as follows:

Students:
I pledge to push for excellence by striving to learn as much as I possibly can. I will work to achieve success in school so that I can prepare myself

for success in life. I will respect the authority of my parents and accept the help of my teachers. I will do everything I can to use my time wisely in order to learn.

Parents:
I pledge to push for excellence by involving myself in the education of my children. I will teach them values and ethics. I will encourage them to develop self-discipline and to learn as much as they can in school and at home. I will teach my children the importance of self-respect and respect for their teachers, and I will require respect for my authority as their parents.

Teachers:
I pledge to push for excellence by using all means available to me to insure that my students achieve excellence in their careers and adult lives. I will motivate students to value knowledge and view it as vital to their futures. I will promote discipline and respect for parents. I will support the efforts of other teachers, parents and students in the pursuit of excellence through devotion to learning (*PUSH for Excellence*, n.d., 4).

The idea of respect for moral authority was central to these pledges, and the use of the pledge as a touchstone to the PUSH/Excel program was similar to patriotic rituals, such as the Pledge of Allegiance to the Flag. It is also similar to the pledge a convert takes upon joining a Baptist church, when the new member pledges to abide by the rules of the church, not to drink alcohol, and to lead a life for Christ.

The first PUSH/Excel publication suggested that parents set rules limiting television viewing so that students could study and engage in discussions with their parents. It said that parents should select television programs, enforce curfews, and stay in contact with school authorities, especially to detect and deal with drug abuse. Parents should have an influence on the friends their children select, and they should establish dress codes that deemphasize sex. Jackson's discipline was Calvinistic in both tone and content. At one high school he said, "There's another side to it, sisters. If you are to deserve the kind of man you cheer for, you cannot spend more time in school on the cultivation of your bosom than your books. If you are to be the right kind of woman, you cannot have a fully developed bottom and a half developed brain. A donkey got an ass, but he ain't got no sense" (Stone 1979, 138).

The second part of the program was to provide role models for students so they could see individuals who had achieved excellence through hard work and against long odds—athletes, business leaders, government officials, blacks from all walks of life who had accomplished much. The first PUSH/Excel booklet suggested that these role models should be invited to speak to school assemblies, and students were encouraged to study their biographies. The Witness for Excellence Program would feature inspirational speakers to motivate excellence in thought as well as in action. Finally, older students could serve as role models for younger ones; the power of peer influence would turn toward the pursuit of excellence rather than the pursuit of pleasure.

Students, the booklet said, needed to be taught that academic success produced success in the world of work and greater satisfaction in life. The booklet suggested that career education programs should be set up to make that connection visible. Parents should become involved in extracurricular student activities like athletics, clubs, and music programs, and students themselves should be involved in governing the school. They should work in community organizations and undertake community improvement projects. Moreover, parents should reward their children for good performance by expressing pride in their accomplishments and through others, more tangible rewards. Schools and communities should provide incentives for academic achievement, such as prizes donated by local businesses. The schools were instructed to make use of the media to convey the PUSH/Excel message clearly and dramatically. Specially written plays, school assemblies, and field trips could communicate the theme of excellence.

This early blueprint for the program stated that PUSH/Excel was not only a program but a philosophy of life. Commitment, discipline, and the assertion of moral authority were the dominant themes. Still, although the first booklet provided an assortment of suggestions for activities, the schools demanded more specific suggestions about how to proceed. A second booklet was produced, that outlined six steps toward mass involvement of parents, pupils, preachers, teachers, and the media, all of which formed the core of a local Excel program.

1. *STATE OF THE SCHOOL ADDRESS.* At the start of each school year the principal should give a state of the school address, setting the climate and the goals for the year. The principal must be the moral authority, teach discipline and academic achievement; and development will be the by-product.
2. *STUDENT PLEDGES.* Students must pledge to commit themselves to study every school-day night a minimum of two hours from 7 to 9 P.M., with the television, radio and record player off and no telephone interruptions. If we match our effort and discipline in athletics in the academic arena, we will achieve the same results.
3. *PARENT PLEDGES.* Parents must pledge to accept responsibility to monitor their child's study hours, and agree to go to school to pick up their child's report card each grading period.
4. *TEACHER PLEDGES.* Teachers must pledge to make meaningful homework assignments; to collect, grade and return homework to students; and call the parent if a student is absent two days in a row or is doing poorly in

school—all of which reflects increased expectations of students on the part of teachers.

5. *WRITTEN ETHICAL CODE OF CONDUCT.* A written ethical code of conduct which presents alternative life styles to drugs, alcohol, violence, teenage pregnancy and other forms of decadence that detract from an educational atmosphere, must be implemented.

6. *VOTER REGISTRATION.* On graduation day all eligible seniors would receive a diploma in one hand (symbolizing knowledge and wisdom), and a voter registration card in the other (symbolizing power and responsibility), as well as given nonpartisan information on how to vote and operate a voting machine (*PUSH for Excellence: The Developing Process of Implementation,* n.d.).

The principal of the school was to serve as moral leader, to set the moral tone of the school, just as the preacher was the moral authority who set the moral tone for the church. Symbols and rituals, such as pledges, state-of-the-school addresses, and graduation ceremonies, played an important role in this approach. The written ethical code of conduct was suggested by political sources, such as the U.S. Constitution, as well as the procedures of the Baptist church. Just as the civil rights movement applied a religious and moral approach to the political goal of black liberation, Jackson's program applied these methods to the goals of education. In Jackson's words, "Only a revival of moral authority, self-discipline and an effort of total involvement will make a difference. That, in a sentence, is the goal and program of PUSH for Excellence" (*PUSH for Excellence,* n.d., 2).

The ideal program would have strong leadership and community support, commitment from school personnel, parent participation, church involvement, teachers with high expectations, access to the media, and money. Jackson did not forget the importance of the media and money, for these were lessons he had learned well. He not only emphasized the necessity of total community commitment and support but also included the church as a major institutional part of the program. The church would provide the necessary moral authority, along with the parents and the school; the three institutions working together would form a tripod of moral support for the child, just as Jackson had experienced it in his own youth in South Carolina. A child who misbehaved in school could be punished at home by his parents and publicly chastised by the preacher in church—just as young Jackson was. The school, the parents, and the church encapsulated the child, and, together, prevented misdirection.

One of Jackson's biographers described the southern black community:

Southern black communities were communal in a literal sense. For the most part this is still true today. Children do not grow up through happenstance as they so often do in Northern urban areas. There is a life plan for them interwoven through the institutions of church, home, and school. Social mores were such that when Jesse was disruptive in class, he was disciplined at school, "whupped" at home, and the preacher—that autocratic figure who dictated to the community—would publicly rebuke Jesse in church. When Jesse presented a severe behavioral problem, it was not unusual for the preacher and his teachers to converge on Jesse at his home.

All three institutions, interlocking, reinforcing, and smoothing out the rough edges, were the crucible of his development as a leader. His school environs offered him the laboratory he needed to test himself, to compete and to measure his achievements (Reynolds 1975, 32).

In the PUSH/Excel scheme every person was assigned specific tasks to perform. Parents should monitor study hours, exchange telephone numbers with teachers, and pick up report cards and test scores from school. Teachers should convey high expectations, expect good behavior and quality work from students, communicate with parents, and assign meaningful homework. Churches should mobilize parents, provide spiritual leadership, fund scholarships, begin tutoring programs, publicly recognize student achievement, and "adopt" schools. Businesses should provide jobs, job training, and scholarships, donate money toward the school programs, and contribute services. Even the media had an assignment—to publicize Excel, help with public relation campaigns, and make financial contributions.

Jackson by then had an ambivalent attitude toward the media. He had ascended to power with its support, but he also saw it as pernicious. "The mass media is the new primary educator in our society because it is the primary transmitter of knowledge, mores, folkways, values, and social trends. . . . What is being programmed into our children's minds through the media? . . . Our children are being programmed into premature heat, and the results are a teenage-pregnancy epidemic and rampant venereal disease" (Jackson 1978, 199–200). His solution was to control and use the media to support his own objectives. Not surprisingly, the media did not emphasize this part of his crusade.

If all these practices were followed, the student would be embedded in a web of high expectations and support that was mutually reinforced by the whole environment. With such "total involvement," the student would be immersed in school, church, and family, shielded from the destructive enticements of a materialistic society, focused toward achievement and accomplishment, on the road to self-respect and excellence. The ultimate PUSH/Excel goal was expressed this way: "Knowledge is the key to power, and power is a basic requirement to achieve progress" (Jackson 1987, 183).

The PUSH/Excel program was much more than a casual idea conceived by Jackson in an instant. It was an expression of his life, reflecting his own understanding of how he got to be where he was—one of the most powerful men in the United States—while all around him in the streets of the ghetto he could see black alcoholics, black drug addicts, black failure. Achievement in school and support by his family and his church had been the reasons for his own success, and he was determined that it would work for others. He sought to recreate for black teenagers the conditions of his own astounding achievement—the warm support of the southern black community.

When he said things like "You're not a man because you can make a baby. They can make babies through artificial insemination. Imbeciles can make babies. Fools can make babies. You're a man only if you can raise a baby, protect a baby and provide for a baby" (Stone 1979, 137), he was not merely moralizing. He was speaking out of his own deeply felt childhood experiences. To bring about the changes he envisioned, Jackson turned to the proven tactics he had learned in the civil rights movement and in his own campaign for economic rights—the mass rally, the demonstration march, community organizing, symbols and rituals, and the use of the mass media to convey his ideals.

A PUSH/Excel School

How were these ideas translated into local programs? The original Excel program was begun in ten high schools in Chicago. Each school tried different activities and had different results. One of the first schools to initiate the program was Manley High School, a school of 2,000 students, all black, located on the West Side, one of the poorest areas of the city. The school administrators were particularly concerned about class attendance and teenage pregnancies; in addition, they hoped to increase the involvement of the local business community in school affairs (American Institutes for Research 1979).

In 1979 Manley established a community advisory council, which collected 1,500 pledges from students and 400 pledges from parents. That fall four busloads of students attended a Reproductive Health and Careers conference at McCormick Place sponsored by PUSH/Excel, and all Chicago PUSH/Excel schools were invited. At Manley, this conference was followed up by six assemblies for the entire student body, whether pledged or unpledged, on reproductive health. One Saturday morning, Manley students visited Operation PUSH headquarters to receive awards for excellence in athletics and academics in front of the entire PUSH assembly. Jackson spoke at the school's National Honor Society Induction, and the top students from Manley participated in an Academic Olympics against other West Side schools. In the spring, students and teachers from Manley participated in a PUSH/Excel Convocation March along with students from other PUSH/Excel schools.

The Manley championship basketball team attended an Excel-A-Thon week in Los Angeles, paid for by Excel, which included visits to Los Angeles high schools, Disneyland, and Hollywood. Excel also participated in the annual athletic awards banquet at the high school. In May, Excel sponsored a voter registration drive to register all eighteen year olds. Some of these PUSH/Excel activities at Manley were sponsored solely by Excel; others were regular school activities. At the end of the year the principal of the school thought attendance was up and pregnancies down, although no formal evaluation was conducted (American Institutes for Research 1979).

Manley High School was one of the most active early Excel schools. Most participating schools had fewer activities, but most had several, and no two school programs were exactly alike. Other Chicago schools organized essay contests, bake sales, ski trips, human relations groups, special choir performances, and band competitions. Los Angeles schools set up teenage health conferences, a PUSH/Excel-A-Thon, a council on violence, job referrals, newsletters, tardy "sweeps," camping trips, and peer counseling. The fact that activities were not uniform across all schools and sites eventually plagued the program in the government-funded AIR evaluation.

Even in schools with many activities, the activities were largely motivational in nature and focused on one-time events. There was no sharp dividing line between regular school activities and those of Excel; no school did everything that the national office suggested, and none followed the guidelines exactly. The Excel program was more like what a Baptist minister would call a "program" for the church—a set of disparate activities, loosely coordinated and designed; it was a flurry of activity rather than a precisely planned pattern of events.

The Decentralized Model

Faced with such diversity and their own civil rights background, the national staff members backed away from a fully centralized operation. With this decentralized approach still in operation, the development of an "organizational model" for local programs was the next step in Excel's evolution. This model was predicated upon close collaboration between school districts and local PUSH/Excel staff. A local PUSH/Excel site director, hired by the national office but housed in offices near the particular school district, would be responsible for local fund-raising, providing liaison with the national office, coordinating interschool activities, and providing technical assistance to program staff in schools. Local community liaisons, in the employ of the national staff but based in each participating school, would work to involve parents and the community in activities such as PUSH/Excel events, report card pickups, tutoring, and job placements. The community liaisons would also select the school advisory council, which would include students, teachers, parents, and community representatives. Each school would also have a teacher-advisor to work with students.

At the district level, an administrator appointed as district program director would be given overall responsibility for the in-school program. The district person and the PUSH/Excel counterpart were to work closely together to coordinate decision making and share responsibility for overall program operations. This cooperative approach assumed the willingness of school districts to give nondistrict personnel a major voice in school affairs and to commit district resources to the support PUSH/Excel's concept of total community involvement.

The national office expected local staff to use this organizational structure, as well as Jackson's ten principles and six core activities, to develop their own programs. This decentralized approach was consistent with "movement" building in the civil rights tradition. It was assumed that local people were in a better position than the national staff to take advantage of the local context in devising a program. The idea was that Jackson's message provided a starting point and the mass rally provided the initial audience. It was up to local staff to work creatively to develop a program that would sustain the commitment of the students and the community. Local sites could receive help from the national office but could not expect the national staff to solve their problems for them. They could call on Jackson when needed, but he would come for only a few days.

In summary, the content of the program was primarily moral; the goal was to reestablish moral authority and self-respect. Students were encouraged to improve their characters, to work hard, behave themselves, stay off drugs, stay out of trouble, respect their parents, help their peers, listen to their ministers, and take pride in their race. Achievement and excellence in academics, in athletics, and in all phases of life, they were told, would follow.

The form of the program followed religious models. Students, parents, and teachers were to pledge themselves to specific goals. The methods were similar to church rituals, reminiscent of converts stepping forward in a Baptist church to commit their lives to Christ. The initial experience would be a mass rally led by one of the greatest preachers in the land, similar in form to a revival. In a traditional tent revival the itinerant preacher calls forth those who would be saved; they step forward and commit themselves, just as in a PUSH/Excel rally. The PUSH/Excel conception of change was that of conversion, of changing one's life in one swift action, in one moment of personal decision. After an evangelical conversion it is up to the home church to receive the new converts and to sustain them in the life of the church. The converts sign a written pledge and are formally inducted into the church, symbolized by immersion in water to wash away their sins. The evangelist is a motivator; the local people must provide the long-term sustenance. This practice was similar to Jackson's notion of PUSH/Excel.

The essence of the program was symbolic; people were motivated by their attachment to powerful symbols. Their conversion was emotional, "straight from the heart." Black teenagers could see a professional football player, could talk to him, could be persuaded that success was possible, that hard work would pay off. Black lawyers, doctors, and businesspeople had the same effect. If one studied hard, success was possible. Jackson saw himself as a programmer of dramas for other people to enact. It was his job to set the stage and create the scenes for people to act out. To motivate people, Jackson employed the symbols of the black church—the preacher, the revivals, the music—and the symbols of the dominant secular culture—big name entertainers, athletes, and politicians—in short, fame and money. Blacks could succeed in a white-dominated world if they worked hard and kept their wits about them. PUSH/Excel was not an educational program with teaching methods or curriculum materials. It was not a program of technique at all. It was a program of symbols.

4

School Politics

Chicago

Chicago was the site of the first PUSH/Excel program. Operation PUSH approached the Chicago Board of Education in 1976 and asked permission to start Excel in several schools. In 1977 activities were begun in ten high schools. Selection of the particular schools was determined by district superintendents and participating principals. Some schools were volunteered by their principals; others were selected by the district superintendents.[1]

In some ways Chicago was the logical place to begin an Excel program. It was the home base of Jesse Jackson and Operation PUSH. Moreover, the Chicago school system had a large number of black students and most of the problems any big city faced. But it had also been declared by Martin Luther King to be the most segregated city in the north, and therein resided potential difficulties. Jackson had spearheaded King's campaign against segregated housing in Chicago in the mid-1960s, a campaign that had faltered against Daley's political machine. Jackson had stayed on in Chicago and had attacked the Chicago political establishment in many different ways. He had organized campaigns, had run for mayor, and as mentioned earlier, had even succeeded in unseating Daley's political delegation at the 1972 Democratic Convention. Jackson was not popular in the mayor's office, to say the least, and even after Daley's death he continued to be unpopular with the established officials. He now asked the Chicago schools for their cooperation in implementing his new educational reform.

Traditionally, the general superintendent of the Chicago schools had been the mayor's man; he had always been a man, and a white man at that—another issue on which Jackson regularly campaigned. The mayor did not appoint the superintendent but did appoint some school board members and influenced the others. Although the board was supposedly nonpolitical, the mayor had always maintained control of it as well as the superintendent of schools.

At this time the main issue for the schools was desegregation. One could draw a line through a map of Chicago and on one side the schools would be 90 percent black and on the other 90 percent white—a segregation that had been maintained for decades. Because this de facto segregation was under attack by the federal government and the state of Illinois, the superintendent had proposed a voluntary desegregation plan called "Access to Excellence." But no one was very happy with this plan, and in the forefront of the opposition was Jesse Jackson.

When PUSH/Excel requested permission to operate in the Chicago schools, the school administration agreed to cooperate. However, because of a shortage of funds, the schools could provide virtually no assistance. The administration adopted a passive attitude, watching the Excel activities from the sidelines but offering no help. If PUSH/Excel wanted to change the schools, they would have to do so without the district's help. The superintendent's rhetoric was supportive; his actions were not. Any innovation has a difficult time succeeding in the public schools, even with the support of the central administration, and it is a maxim among those who study school change that support of the central school administration is critical to the success of a new program (Fullan 1982).

Nonetheless, Excel forged ahead, and there were enough interested people in the schools to provide some basis for support. The first PUSH/Excel director was Reginald Brown, principal of Chicago Vocational High School, who continued his duties as principal while directing the initial efforts. Brown was highly regarded in Chicago; he succeeded in obtaining a grant of $102,000 from the Chicago Community Trust. In the fall of 1977 Carl Boyd became the first full-time Chicago director. He initiated several activities, such as Adopt-a-School, Ministers for Excellence, Academic Olympics, Parents for Excellence, and Athletes for Excellence. (American Institutes for Research 1979).

Because of the school district's lack of support, however, PUSH/Excel staff members could not be located inside the schools. They had to operate from PUSH headquarters with school principals serving as their main contacts. The program received $255,000 from the Illinois Family Planning Council to combat teenage pregnancy, and in 1979 the Chicago and Kansas City programs received $500,000 from the U.S. Department of Labor for a Career Exploration Demonstration Project. Early in 1979 the Reverend William Samuels became the next director of the Chicago program. His staff consisted of an assistant director, a parenting director, a youth coordinator, a liaison chief, a special consultant, and a secretary. Meanwhile, Dr. Donald Thompson was appointed director of the national office.

It's Gonna Get Killed

The Illinois state superintendent of schools was Joseph Cronin. As state superintendent, Cronin had two huge gripes with Chicago. One involved civil rights. Cronin had a strong personal commitment to civil rights and equal educational opportunities, and Chicago, where a large portion of the state's children attended school, had repeatedly violated desegregation mandates over the years. Cronin had a strong endorsement from the Illinois State Board of Education to pursue civil rights aggressively. The second major problem Cronin encountered was how to do anything at all in Chicago. Although legally the city was accountable to the state in educational matters, the state traditionally had little authority in Chicago. The state agency had been effectively frozen out of the Chicago schools for decades. Long before Cronin arrived in Illinois, state officials had trundled up and down the dark corridors of the massive Board of Education building, being shunted from office to office. No one seemed to be responsible for anything in the central office (Dixon 1983).

Cronin was especially frustrated with Chicago's desegregation plan. The plan had been drawn up by a task force of four city officials and four state officials. They met and discussed the issue, and the Chicago representatives wrote the report. When the state officials saw the report, they wondered whether they had really agreed to what was on paper. They were assured that their concern was only a matter of interpretation, but when the report was made public, it was interpreted the way the state officials had feared. "The Chicago schools had the best professional writers in town," one participant said (Dixon 1983). What the state officials objected to was that the plan allowed for too much voluntarism.

Cronin and the state were not without power. Legally they could cut off state aid to the city. They had already actually cut $5 million in vocational funds earlier, but cutting off all state aid—$400 million— would be equivalent to dropping the atomic bomb. The weapon was simply too destructive to use. "Too many zero's," Cronin said. Too many students, too many people, too many dollars (Dixon 1983). At one time the U.S. Office of Education had been bold enough to cut off federal funds to Chicago, but that had lasted only until the mayor called then President Lyndon Johnson.

So when Cronin and his staff read the announcement about federal support for PUSH/Excel, they had two reactions. The first was that here was an excellent opportunity for the state to do something about black education in Chicago. PUSH/Excel had gained access to the Chicago schools in a way the state of Illinois had not been able to do. Cronin called in Daniel Dixon, his top black advisor. Dixon was bright, highly articulate, a longtime Chicago resident, and a shrewd observer of Chicago politics. His title was manager of special projects, which meant that he was close to both Cronin and Deputy Superintendent Nelson Ashline and could circumvent the state bureaucracy, with their approval.

Cronin and Dixon were in complete agreement about PUSH/Excel: "It's going to get killed in the evaluation" (Dixon 1983). Both men had extensive experience dealing with the federal government. Dixon had been state liaison for the "disadvantaged" in the Title I Elementary and Secondary Education Act (ESEA) program in Chicago, and he knew what the federal evaluations were like. PUSH/Excel did not have a traditional educational component, and it was not likely to clear the federal hurdles. "We knew what was going to happen to Excel. Joe Cronin predicted it; I predicted. We said it's gonna fall," Dixon said. Cronin said, "It seems to me that there's not an educational component in the traditional sense, and they're getting set up for a rip off." The PUSH/Excel people seemed unaware of the danger.

Cronin and Dixon reasoned that the thing to do was to tie the Excel program to in-school activities. Cronin had been touting something called Responsibility Education, and his office had developed citizenship activities, such as mock elections, which were meant to foster civic responsibility. If the evaluation could be focused toward addressing such things as the number of high school students registered to vote, Excel might have a chance in the evaluation. Another alternative would be for Excel to hook up with a standardized school program. Title IV, ESEA, provided a procedure by which educational programs could be "nationally validated" by the federal government. If Excel was associated with one of these previously validated programs, they reasoned, federal evaluators could hardly declare it a failure. "Intertwine those two and there'd be no way an external evaluator of the federal ilk could come in here and say Excel is not worth its salt," Dixon said.

Excited by the prospects of cooperation, Cronin and Dixon chartered a plane and flew to Cleveland to talk to Jackson, who was attending the annual PUSH conference there. They offered him state assistance in program development and in expanding the PUSH/Excel program in Illinois. Jackson was interested and wanted to cooperate. Within a short time the entire Chicago staff journeyed to Springfield for a meeting that lasted an entire day. The Illinois state agency presented the range of services it could offer; the Excel people listened patiently and said they would be in touch. They never followed up. Similar cooperation was offered by other groups, with similar results (Dixon 1983).

Jonah and the Whale

Meanwhile the PUSH/Excel staff employees were inundated with the details of running the program in Chicago. Trying to manage the enterprise from their offices at Operation PUSH, they collected pledges, organized parents, talked to community leaders, established school programs, and raised money. The phone in their office rang fifteen times an hour with a constant deluge of details. If there was a parents' meeting that night, whoever was available went to give the speech. There was little role definition for performing various tasks, and most of the work was crisis management. The staff was spread too thin and became entangled in the details of working with only a few schools. Organizational problems that had always plagued Operation PUSH now beset its offspring as well.

The first Chicago director, Reginald Brown, had been a professional educator knowledgeable about the system. Later directors were experienced in working with movements, like the Reverend William Samuels. They were totally committed but forced to work from outside the system and with a limited understanding of the schools. Rather than train indigenous people who might perform the routine tasks on-site, and hence free the central staff for long-range planning and more important tasks, the Excel staff became bogged down with daily routine. Even when they were offered help, they were in no position to take advantage of it. They were attending night meetings and working ten to twelve hours a day already. Excel's problems in Chicago were compounded by the lack of support from the central administration. The school administration offered no overt resistance; neither did it help. According to Dixon, the administration displayed a masterpiece of noncooperation, even by Chicago standards. The Chicago administration reasoned, "We're not gonna have another David and Goliath. More like Jonah and the whale, and we're the whale—you gonna get swallowed" (Dixon 1983).

To have any chance of success Excel needed the active support of at least three of the six layers of the Chicago bureaucracy. The school board was not critical to the program's success, but the general Chicago superintendent was, and he was hostile (Dixon 1983). The support of the central office staff was not essential, but the support of the district superintendents was, and they were neutral on this issue, perhaps because of the general superintendent's attitude. The support of the district staff was not crucial, but the support of the principals was, and that depended on the individual principals. Excel had its greatest successes working with particular principals, and good programs were indeed developed in schools where the principals were enthusiastic.

District superintendents were the worst problem. Perhaps they were under orders from the general superintendent to be unsupportive; at any rate, they often would not allow the program to spread within their districts. Some principals would have loved the program and saw it as a way of gaining community support, according to Dixon. Others saw the establishment of another line of authority, and the sometimes militant behavior of the Excel staff, as a threat to them personally, and resisted the program. Excel worked well in schools where the principal was committed, but ultimately the active support of the general superintendent was critical for the program to succeed, and Excel did not have that.

In the long run the Chicago school system tolerated and finally absorbed PUSH/Excel, as it had so many other reforms over the years. Strenuous though its efforts were, PUSH/Excel could not do the job alone. It needed school authorities from inside the system to push as well, and not even the support of the individual principals was enough. Nor would the support of the general superintendent have been enough without the support of the principals. When help was offered, as from the state agencies, which had agendas of their own, PUSH/Excel was unable or unwilling to take advantage of it. State agencies were yet other bureaucracies with their own rules, regulations, and jargon. "Title I" and "Title IV" and "national validation" were not the language of PUSH/Excel. Dixon later said it was as if the Illinois state agency was "a well-oiled machine trying to interface with PUSH/Excel, but PUSH/Excel did not have the proper gears and clogs to mesh with it."

While the program was becoming mired in Chicago, the politics of the situation demanded that Excel increase its national visibility. In the words of one observer, Jackson floated across the national scene "like a butterfly." National directors of PUSH/Excel came and went; there was little continuity in the management of the program and little communication between them.

Several tendencies were apparent in the Chicago endeavor. Although PUSH/Excel had some good ideas that were able to motivate students, at least in the short run, the selection of Chicago was not the best choice. Jackson had long been at war with the Chicago political establishment, particularly over appointments to the school superintendency, and it was rather naive to expect cooperation. Even though the PUSH staff was hard-working and highly motivated, they did not know how to operate in the public schools. They needed help from inside. Finally, even when help was offered, PUSH was often unable to accept it. They continued to operate in the Chicago schools for years, but it was apparent early that the program was not going very far.

Kansas City

The Kansas City program began at Central High School. As a result of the 1954 *Brown* vs. *Board of Education* decision ending legal school segregation, Central had changed from an all-white school in 1956 to an all-black school in 1963—one of the ironies of desegregation. The school was located in a stable working-class neighborhood of Kansas

City, and even though the transition from white to black was marked by racial tension, the school had managed to maintain high quality in both athletics and academics. Its teams had won several state basketball and track championships in the 1960s, students had won scholastic competitions, and the school was known nationally as one of the finest black high schools in the nation, with many prominent graduates. By the early 1970s, however, the school seemed to be declining in quality. Kamau King, an alumnus, became alarmed and formed a Central High Alumni Association (CAA) in an attempt to reestablish Central's athletic prowess. This revitalization was later expanded to include academics and other aspects of school life (American Institutes for Research 1979).

In 1976 a CAA member told the group about the beginnings of PUSH/Excel in Chicago, and so the CAA invited Jackson to Kansas City. The superintendent of schools, Robert Wheeler, had served previously in Washington and knew Jackson. After Jackson's visit, the CAA prevailed upon the school board to make Central High the pilot school for Excel in Kansas City, and the superintendent recommended that Will MacCarther be the first director. His office was located at Central High, but his salary was paid by the national office.

During 1977–1978 MacCarther organized activities but did not get along well with the national PUSH/Excel office; he resigned in the summer (American Institutes for Research 1979). In the fall of 1978 the national office selected Terry Johnson as acting director until a permanent one could be hired. Johnson continued the parent activities, but the split between the national office and MacCarther had seriously eroded local support. Johnson tried to increase that support, but the Central High principal told him that the school's loyalty had to be with the CAA rather than with Excel and suggested that Johnson curtail Excel activities at Central (American Institutes for Research 1979). So Johnson moved his office off the Central campus and tried to involve other high schools in Kansas City. Another high school was having severe racial difficulties, and he received an invitation from the principal to work there; but the superintendent refused to designate that school as an official PUSH/Excel school, so Johnson continued his work only informally. Central High then invited Johnson back but set limits as to what he could do.

Although the Kansas City school district had endorsed and publicized the Excel activities at Central, it had never put any of its own money into the program. Federal grants and the national office funded the small Kansas City operation. This situation continued until all federal funds were shut off in the early part of the Reagan administration. During its operation, PUSH/Excel in Kansas City remained centered in only one high school, supported by external funds. The district's relations with the national office were never good, and the program remained essentially an adjunct to the CAA activities. It was an active but highly contained program. Again, local school politics, as well as the poor relationship between the national office and the local district, prevented the expansion into something grander.

Los Angeles

Unlike either the Chicago or the Kansas City programs, PUSH/Excel in Los Angeles had the strong support of the central school administration. In 1976 Jackson spoke to the Los Angeles school board, and they voted to appropriate local funds for the 1977-1978 school year—$400,000 for the first year alone. The central administration canvassed the local schools to determine which ones wanted to participate, and nine high schools volunteered, most of them predominantly black (American Institutes of Research 1979).

It was agreed that each participating school would have a governing council, a teacher-advisor, and a community liaison person, and that the program would be headed by a director and a coordinator working within the school district. This organizational structure was eventually adopted for other sites around the country. The initial programs focused on reducing absenteeism and tardiness. During its first year the Los Angeles program was the most successful one in the country, and the national staff pointed to it with pride. The next year things changed, however.

The Proposition 13 budget crisis hit California, and the Los Angeles schools were faced with a loss of $33 million in state aid. At the same time the procedures for electing school board members were changed, and one of PUSH/Excel's supporters lost his reelection bid. Simultaneously, Howard Miller, the president of the school board and one of PUSH/Excel's strongest advocates, was subjected to a recall election. Miller had also supported court-ordered desegregation, which required busing students long distances across town. An irate white citizenry demanded his recall, and he was defeated by Roberta Weintaub, a strong opponent of the busing plan. This development left a school board of three conservatives and three moderate-liberals (S. Murray et al. 1982). One school board seat remained vacant; the board was unable to select a replacement, although it attempted 261 ballots. After 60 ballots to elect a new board president, a compromise was reached in which the new conservative member, Weintaub, became president. When another special election was held, another strong busing opponent was elected, giving the conservatives a 4–3 majority.

Even before the budget crisis, conservative members of the board had opposed PUSH/Excel, and the superintendent of schools had indicated to the Excel director that the funding might be discontinued. So in 1979, the third year of the Los Angeles program, the Excel budget was reduced by half, to $279,000. In 1980 when the conservative board took office, school district funds were cut entirely. The program managed to survive another year by receiving $132,000 from the federal grant funds to the national office, $274,113 from the federal CETA program, and $71,000 in private contributions. However, in the summer of 1981 the program ceased to operate altogether.

Support for the program remained high at the middle level of the district administration and in the participating schools. The school district conducted its own evaluation and concluded that attendance had improved and absenteeism had been reduced. Staff in the participating schools thought the program a success. In fact, the internal district evaluation report recommended that the program be continued, but all that was swept aside by the changes in the composition of the school board.

Los Angeles had gone from being the most highly regarded PUSH/Excel program in 1977 to a nonexistent program in 1981. This turnabout had been the result of sweeping changes in school board politics brought about by white reaction to desegregation by busing. Jackson's program was one of the first casualties. The fact that it was Calvinistic in content, moralistic in tone, and kept blacks in their own schools did not matter. The reason given for the demise of the program was lack of funds. PUSH/Excel fought back by trying to obtain money directly from the governor. Governor Jerry Brown was close to using his own discretionary funds to support the Los Angeles program—the request for funds was on his desk awaiting his signature—when Jesse Jackson made his fateful trip to the Middle East. The governor decided at the last moment not to endorse the request (S. Murray et al. 1982).

Jackson's Trip to the Middle East

Then Jesse Jackson went to the Middle East. In September 1979 he made front-page news by being photographed embracing Palestine Liberation Organization leader Yasser Arafat. The story sent shock waves reverberating through PUSH/Excel communities. Jackson's debut into international politics was unanimously censured by the American press, by public opinion, and particularly by the American Jewish community. His trip proved particularly ill fated and ill timed for PUSH/Excel. Why did he go?

Early in 1979 Andrew Young, ambassador to the United Nations and the highest-ranking U.S. black official, had met secretly with a representative of the terrorist Palestine Liberation Organization. When word leaked out, there was a tremendous outcry from the public, particularly the American Jewish community, which demanded his ouster. Under pressure, President Carter dismissed Young. This move in turn outraged the black community, who rallied to Young's support. Throughout the year various black leaders took up the cause, and in the fall Joseph Lowery of the Southern Christian Leadership Conference led a delegation of ten prominent black leaders to the Middle East to meet with the PLO. Their trip received only modest publicity (Landess and Quinn 1985).

Jackson then announced that he too was traveling to the Middle East to meet with Arafat, and his visit received much publicity, culminating in the photograph of him embracing Arafat, which appeared on front pages of newspapers across the country on September 30, 1979. Although this incident was not related directly to PUSH/Excel, it created tremendous problems for the national office and local programs. Reflecting on the trip's impact in an interview in 1980, AIR PUSH/Excel evaluator Saundra Murray observed:

> It all began in Memphis in a meeting with the school board in October of '79. They had been quite supportive, but when Jackson went to the Middle East, they wanted me to provide an elaborate explanation of the program and what it was accomplishing. I think they wanted me to say, "The program stinks," but I didn't. Jackson's trip got a lot of publicity in the Memphis papers, and the superintendent, who had been in favor of it, withdrew his support. PUSH/Excel never even got to a board vote. The superintendent was presenting his desegregation plans to the board, and he didn't want anything controversial around at that time.
>
> I think Memphis never got started because of his trip. That caused us a lot of trouble in several sites. The evidence that the problem in Memphis was due to the trip to the Middle East is all circumstantial; no one ever said it outright, but it's pretty clear.
>
> There was also considerable concern in Denver about his trip. We got a lot of flack from the Jewish community. People were saying, "Why should taxpayers support this program when Jackson is so political?" Ruth Hornby on the national staff was very concerned about it as well. She apparently spoke to Jackson about it, but the national staff won't admit it or, if they do, say what was said during the conversation.

In discussing Murray's comment that "no one ever said it outright," Norman Gold of the National Institute of Education said, "Bullshit. People were saying it right out" (Gold 1980).

Jackson's trip also abruptly terminated Excel's prospects in Louisiana; the state legislature quickly cancelled its grant to New Orleans. "I'm not sure that was the only reason, but he seemed not to be very popular with our legislature that year," said Marie Langly. "People acted as if they were afraid to touch it" (Smith 1982). And Saundra Murray reported that in Chattanooga the superintendent and his staff "gave us quite a hard time over the evaluation" because of the Middle East trip. The matter finally quieted down there, as local Excel board member Ruth Holmberg, publisher of the *Chattanooga Times* and an "integral member of the Chattanooga power structure," reportedly kept local funders "in line" (Hendrix 1981; Witherspoon 1981). Perhaps coincidentally, Jackson's trip received scant attention in the local Chattanooga press, unlike elsewhere.

Some people thought that the Middle East trip was designed for publicity. Others believed that Jackson was setting a good example for students by speaking out on controversial issues. But whatever the motivation, the trip had disastrous consequences for PUSH/Excel. It cooled the enthusiasm of school districts and former supporters and further strained relations between local programs and the national office. Those running local programs already felt the national office was not providing enough assistance, and they didn't need this bad publicity on top of already serious problems. PUSH/Excel depended on local contributors to donate money. Those funds now dwindled.

Before the trip Jackson's own advisors had warned him that such a course of action would cost him Jewish support, but Jackson followed his own dictates. Perhaps he was also intent on establishing Arab contacts. Robert Abboud, president of the First National Bank of Chicago and the most prominent Chicagoan of Arab descent, was tutoring inner city youths in the Greek classics. Shortly before the trip Abboud held a luncheon for dignitaries to showcase his prize students and to demonstrate that these students could learn anything if given a chance. A Jewish organization had offered to support the expansion of the tutoring program in Chicago under PUSH/Excel sponsorship. A week after the Middle East trip all the offers had been withdrawn.[2]

The entire affair seriously exacerbated relations between American blacks and American Jews in general and between Jackson and the Jewish community in particular. Five years later these relations would be rubbed raw once again by Jackson's "Hymietown" remarks and his association with black Muslim leader Louis Farrakhan. Jackson's own explanation of his Middle East trip was that it was his responsibility to serve as a role model for black youth by standing up for what he believed in regardless of the political consequences.

Whatever Jackson's motivation and whatever the long-term consequences, the immediate effects on the program were catastrophic. The Memphis and New Orleans programs were stillborn. All PUSH/Excel programs suffered severe losses of financial and political support. Even though Jackson's trip had nothing to do with education directly, it dealt PUSH/Excel a stunning blow from which it never fully recovered. Of course, it was not the first time that ethnic politics had seriously affected education. School politics are often ethnic politics.

Notes

1. The Chicago school system was organized into twenty-seven separate districts, each headed by a district superintendent, who in turn was accountable to the school board.

2. Apparently what hurt Jackson most was the highly publicized photograph of him and Arafat embracing. Arafat is smiling joyously, tucking his head into Jackson's neck. Jackson is also smiling but cooler; both men have their arms around each other. This photo aroused the ire of many people, and some PUSH/Excel supporters spoke bitterly of Jackson's "love for Arafat." As with so many of Jackson's actions, the entire episode was primarily symbolic. No deals were struck; no agreements drawn. But the photo rankled people and was not forgotten. It appeared and was referred to in the press many times when Jackson ran for president in 1984 and 1988.

5

An Inside Look at Two Programs

After the demise of the short-lived Los Angeles program, the best PUSH/Excel sites were those in Denver and Chattanooga, in the opinion of several federal officials. The program in Denver began when Omar Blair, a black community leader and president of the Board of Education, visited Central High in Kansas City, his alma mater. He said in an interview (1981) that he thought that Excel had "turned the school around" and that he had invited Jackson to Denver in hopes of initiating PUSH/Excel there. In 1978 Blair gained acceptance for the program by the Denver school board, and the program began in August 1979.

Four schools were selected by the central administration to initiate the program. At least two of the principals clearly had reservations, and only one had volunteered his school. The principals were then asked to select their own teacher-advisors. Before the program began, there was disagreement between the school district and the national office over how the Denver program should be organized. The original plan called for a dual governing structure, with the PUSH people in control of both the community liaisons and the teacher-advisors. However, after much negotiation, the Denver central office insisted on being totally in charge of the program inside the schools, presumably because they did not want outsiders to share authority for the program. The PUSH/Excel director had to report to the school district coordinator, even though he and the teacher-advisors were paid by the national office in Chicago. Furthermore, the PUSH office was located off school district property, supposedly to allow them to work better with community groups. This authority structure ultimately plagued the program (Hamilton 1981).

The first Excel director was Paul Hamilton, a teacher at Manual High School who had been active in civil rights and elected to the state legislature at the age of twenty-five. He was committed, militant, and reportedly difficult for school authorities to get along with; furthermore, he had firm ideas about what should be done. Hamilton was to report both to the national office and to the director of Pupil Personnel Services, Evie Dennis. Unlike Hamilton, Dennis was a team player, and her attitude was, "I just get handed these sorts of programs by the super-intendent, who doesn't know what else to do with them" (Dennis 1981). She had many programs in her purview, and although she was black, PUSH/Excel seemed much like the others. However, she did worry that it might cause trouble because of Jackson's controversial reputation. She and Hamilton were on different tracks—the district team player versus the community activist.

Jackson kicked off the Denver program with a rally in September 1979. Unfortunately, he arrived one day before leaving for the Middle East, and the local press gave far more attention to his politics than to PUSH/Excel. The Middle East trip caused immense problems with Denver funding. The first year the program was supported with $74,670 in federal money, $24,875 in district money, and $89,000 in local contributions (S. Murray et al. 1982). After Jackson's trip, local contributors started withdrawing their support.

Jesse Jackson and Joseph Coors

The most prominent businessman to object to Jackson's trip to the Middle East was Joseph Coors, owner of Coors Brewery and supporter of arch-conservative causes. The Coors Foundation had contributed $100,000 to the Denver PUSH/Excel operation, but after the Middle East trip, Coors threatened to withdraw it. He saw no reason why he should support the teaching of Jackson's politics in the public schools (Blair 1981, Hamilton 1981; Radefsky 1981). The program staff finally persuaded Coors that the Denver program was independent of the national operation, and Coors allowed his contribution to remain, pro-vided the independence of the Denver program was demonstrated. Other businesspeople had similar reactions.

The fund-raisers also faced opposition from the local Jewish community, and potential contributors raised questions about Jackson's "love for Arafat." One fund-raiser said it was unfortunate that so many questions about the program were political rather than educational (Radefsky 1981). Hamilton was told that he needed to find "a white man, preferably a Jew because of Jesse's politics, to head the effort" to raise funds. Eventually, he managed to convince Sydney Friedman, a vice president of the Samsonite corporation, to chair the fund-raising committee. The strategy the Denver fund-raisers employed was to disassociate themselves from Jackson. They tried to persuade potential contributors that PUSH/Excel was not an attempt "to overthrow the U.S. government," and it took a good deal of effort to convince them of the autonomy of the Denver program. Denver leaders decided not to invite Jackson back for a second visit, as had been planned.

In the beginning Hamilton expected help from the national office on how to proceed, but no help was forthcoming. His superior had authority over the program in the district, the principals had authority over the program in their schools, but no one had any notion of what to do or how to begin. Some teacher-advisors in the schools did have ideas, but those ideas were often vetoed by the principals. No one was certain how to proceed.

Meanwhile, Hamilton encountered resistance when he began to emphasize community involvement in the schools. In his view, the school district was basically resistant to community participation. When he tried to organize parents meetings, the principals objected that he was organizing parents against the schools. He was told not to organize parents and not to work with the Concerned Citizens Congress, a group that had been highly critical of the schools. Faced with the problems of Jackson's image, declining contributions and resistance from the school district, Hamilton resigned as director. He said, "I spent so much time raising money that I didn't have time to administer PUSH/Excel (Hamilton 1981).

East High School

The principal of East High School, John Astuno, had actually wanted to have PUSH/Excel in his school. His student body was 40 percent black. He had heard Jackson speak, and he thought "he is good." If the program had money and would help kids, then he wanted it, whatever its name. The principal had a reputation for taking controversial stands, and even though Jackson had a reputation among white parents as "a flashy person out for the bucks," the principal thought he could handle the potential conflict (Astuno 1981).

However, Willard Smith, the teacher-advisor at East, reported in an interview in 1981 that when he tried to organize events, the principal was hard to please. Smith developed an overall plan for the school three times, and each plan was rejected. In addition, Smith was not allowed to meet with student pledges during school time. Smith was allowed to use his "administrative period," fifteen minutes once a week, for such purposes, but in Smith's view that was not enough time to accomplish anything. The principal then suggested meeting with the pledges in one big assembly, but during the time assigned—8 A.M. on a Monday morning—only 40 of the 300 pledges showed up. When the principal discovered that Smith had complained to the school advisory group about the lack of administrative support, he was outraged. A teacher-advisor who later replaced Smith at East, Dianne Houghtaling, had no respect for the PUSH/Excel staff and saw herself directly under the principal's control (Houghtaling 1981).

The principal also felt that the community liaison, Michael Welsh, was organizing parents against him and barred her from working in the school altogether (Astuno 1981). In Welsh's opinion, none of the Denver schools accepted the community involvement aspect of the program. She had arranged for tutors, free music lessons, and volunteer workers from the community, but these services were never used because the teacher-advisors didn't know the students well enough to know who could benefit from them. "Basically we have been told to wait until we are called," she said. She organized a few dinners for the teachers through the community task group, but nothing much came of this strategy either (Welsh 1981).

Nor were meetings among the PUSH/Excel administrators successful in straightening out the difficulties. When Smith heard that Hamilton had resigned as director, Smith quit his teacher-advisor job at East and assumed the director's position. As director, Smith still did not get along well with the principal. This situation, coupled with the fact that the community liaison was barred from entering the school, meant that prospects at East High School were not good.

The chairman of a religious task group formed in Denver thought there was both a lack of cooperation from the principals and a "lack of clarity about what we [were] doing" (Amundsen 1981). The advisory council at East High focused on a school beautification project—"where the trash cans were"—and when the issue of drug abuse in the school was raised, it was made clear that talking about drugs was off limits. But mainly, "Politics has been the big drawback so far because Jesse Jackson is a turn-off for many people. He isn't really needed, and we could certainly carry it off without him" (Amundsen 1981). Whatever their disagreements with each other, all the Denverites tried to disassociate themselves from Jesse Jackson.

Manual High School

The exacerbated relationships like those between the principal and the PUSH/Excel staff at East High did not emerge at Manual High School. However, Manual's principal, Mary Gentile, was cautious about the program because it had no "solid method." People sat around trying to think up ideas but did not know what would work. Teachers at the school resented the program because the teacher-advisors had fewer students to deal with than did the regular teachers. Also, "Federal programs come and go, and the teachers are cynical" (Gentile 1981). This sort of comment is frequently heard about federal programs all around the country.

Gentile also cited the community groups as a source of frustration. At Manual High alone there were community groups required for all federal programs—work-study programs, the Adopt-a-School program, the curriculum advisory committee, the executive intern program, the budget advisory committee, the parent-teacher association, the school accountability project, and a court-ordered human relations committee. These community groups required a great deal of time to maintain. "It is hard to work with them because they don't really understand schools, and most of the time the schools have to keep the committees active. They tend to wander away, but because the committees are required, we spend quite a lot of time scheduling, arranging, developing agendas, and orchestrating meetings," Gentile said.

The teacher-advisor at Manual, Rudy Carey, was a young black man who saw his duties as collecting pledges, monitoring grades and attendance, and arranging for peer and teacher tutoring for those students who needed extra help. He knew the program needed something more, but in his opinion, PUSH/Excel did not contribute toward his own professional development, and furthermore, the teachers did not like Jesse Jackson. The white teachers "bad-mouthed" the program. Nevertheless, he thought that as many as ten students at Manual might have dropped out of school without the program (Carey 1981).

Willard Smith, by now PUSH/Excel director, was unhappy about the teacher-advisors, over whom he had no control. The teacher-advisors worked hard but did more for the principals than for the program. Only one advisor came close to doing what Smith thought was needed. Moreover, the teacher-advisors did not want to attend evening meetings with community groups, claiming that they were certified teachers and teachers didn't do that. The result was that the community liaison personnel had to work with community groups by themselves and there was little coordination between the advisors and the community groups— one of the main strategies of the PUSH/Excel program. Again, Smith was helpless to correct the situation (Smith 1981).

Lack of commitment to the program was a general problem, and those at fault included teacher-advisors, teachers, principals, and the central administration.[1] Evie Dennis said, "You can go into the schools and never see any indication that PUSH/Excel is there—never a sign or poster. I don't know if it's a lack of commitment to the program, or whether the principal feels that she will offend some people by making it visible. But there a few traces of it around" (Dennis 1981). John Bates, a former teacher and Advisory Board member at Manual, cited the voter registration issue as an example of the lack of administrative commitment. The notion of handing out voter registration cards at the Manual High School graduation ceremony, a basic concept of the PUSH/Excel program, was vetoed by the downtown district office because they didn't want the program to seem too political. "What," this person asked, "is too political about registering people to vote in a democracy?" (Bates 1981). The Denver office was nervous about its association with Jesse Jackson and PUSH/Excel.

Authority in the Denver Schools

Jackson had begun PUSH/Excel as a means of reestablishing moral authority in the lives of black teenagers. Ironically, authority in the Denver public schools was distributed in such a way as to prevent the program from ultimately succeeding. There was a lack of direction both from the national office and from the school district itself. The local office had little influence over what occurred in the schools. The president of the school board had introduced PUSH/Excel to the Denver schools, and the administration had received it with lukewarm enthusiasm.

Rather than seek interested schools to participate, district officials ordered certain schools to institute the program. In addition, the school staffs, especially the white teachers, were adamantly opposed to Jackson personally and thought the teacher-advisors got special privileges. The principals had veto power over teacher-advisors and did not want parent and community groups running out of control. Although the local PUSH/Excel office and parent groups tried to rectify the situation through the central office, these attempts were unsuccessful. The teacher-advisors performed routine school duties rather than program duties.

Meanwhile, two developments served to reduce public support. First, Jackson created a furor by his Middle East trip, and prominent citizens withdrew their support for political reasons. The national and local press began to present Jackson in a negative light. The local PUSH/Excel staff tried to disassociate itself from him and succeeded to some degree, arguing that the Denver program was quite autonomous. Nonetheless, the local program suffered from Jackson's politics. The second cause of erosion in support for Excel derived from the election of a new school board. The Denver public had a liberal attitude toward blacks, and the board had successfully desegregated its schools in the 1960s. However, when school enrollments dropped and the middle schools were reorganized, the issue arose again. Pupils were reassigned to schools, and desegregation became an issue in the 1981 school board election. A conservative, antidesegregation school board took office with a majority of 4 to 3. The main PUSH/Excel supporter was deposed as board president, and although no immediate moves were made to eliminate the program, its weakened state and the lack of commitment by the school district made the prognosis bleak. The school administration, meanwhile, was preparing another program that had some of Excel's features but was not associated with Jackson in any way.

In the long run, no single official in Denver had enough authority to make the program work properly, but there was enough opposition to block it. The school board was split on the issue, and the central administration was passive. The principals were at odds with the PUSH/Excel staff, and the teachers in the schools were mostly negative about the program. The local funders were alienated, and community groups were excluded. Everyone involved in the Denver program was trying to keep Jesse Jackson at arms length. Denver's fragmented, pluralistic social structure did not provide a fertile seedbed. The moral authority for the students that PUSH/Excel sought was lost in the pluralism of the schools. As Paul Hamilton, the first local PUSH/Excel director, put it, "The system is one of no authorities."

Chattanooga

On June 11, 1981, an end-of-the-school-year retreat of the Chattanooga PUSH/Excel staff was held at Covenant College, a beautiful site on Lookout Mountain with a spectacular view of the city of Chattanooga. The site was formerly a resort, best known for the place where Eddie Fisher and Elizabeth Taylor spent their honeymoon. Now it is a bit run down but is still attractive, a small religious college with the motto, "In All Things Christ Preeminent," inscribed over the entrance archway.

The 100 or so attending the conference stayed in the "Castle," the old lodge of the resort, and the meetings were held in the auditorium of the new college chapel, a modern lecture room. A group of somberly dressed men and women watched the proceedings silently—black ministers from the local churches who had been invited to attend the meeting. PUSH/Excel staff, mostly teachers from Chattanooga, filled the other seats. The ministers were introduced one by one as honored guests.

The agenda covered the entire range of PUSH/Excel concerns. After the invocation by one of the ministers, the first speaker was Saundra Murray, project director of the American Institutes for Research (AIR) evaluation of PUSH/Excel. All three of the AIR evaluation reports published thus far had been strongly negative about the national PUSH/Excel program, and the Chattanoogans were clearly angry about it. Murray knew she was facing a hostile audience. The third evaluation report had just been released, and Murray was obviously under considerable duress as she spoke. She did not attempt a justification of the evaluation but rather launched straight into a description of the study, presenting AIR's own program rationale. She said that Chattanooga should have conducted a formal "needs assessment" before it started its program, and she wondered whether the original assumptions that the students had poor attitudes and improper role models were really correct. Her presentation was soft, advice-giving, maternal.

The next speaker was Jane Harbaugh, a PUSH/Excel advisory board member and administrator from the local University of Tennessee campus. She admitted to not being an evaluation specialist but presented evidence that attendance and test scores had improved in the school district, counter to the findings of the national evaluation. Saundra Murray spoke up immediately and said that "attributing cause" in an evaluation is a difficult task. Harbaugh countered testily that the criticisms of the program for "one-shot" activities were unfair and that those activities could be very important.

After a coffee break Clifford Hendrix, the assistant superintendent of schools and a force behind the implementation of PUSH/Excel in Chattanooga, talked about the budget crisis in the school district. PUSH/Excel would have to be cut from $15,000 to $10,000 for its field trips and from $6,000 to $3,000 for its recognition ceremonies and awards. The cuts indicated what a modest sum the district had invested into the program. An enthusiastic discussion ensued with everyone in the audience wanting to voice an opinion. What kinds of awards should be given? Should there be awards for slow students? PUSH/Excel was to support school activities, not replace them. Finally, some felt that awards would have no value if too many were given.

This exchange was followed by a presentation by each school staff on the activities their schools had undertaken. The staff from Howard High talked about their Career Day, Martin Luther King Birthday Celebration, the Art and Essay Contest, and their Star Roll Plaques. The Alton Park Junior High School staff talked about its Pushette Club and Black History Month. Each school made a presentation; the activities sounded impressive and inventive, and the response from the audience was lively and enthusiastic.

The next morning Elma Mardis, the national director, arrived to talk about recent developments. The Reagan administration was withholding funds even though Congress had appropriated the money, she said. The funds would be forthcoming, but she didn't know when. The national office had hired Walt Disney Productions to produce some supplementary classroom materials and had also commissioned the development of a management information system. All of these actions were in direct response to criticisms by the AIR evaluators. Mardis even discussed "stakeholders," a concept taken directly from the evaluation reports. "Stakeholders" are defined as people who have a direct interest in the program and who were presumed to be the major audience for the evaluation reports. Apparently, the evaluation had influenced the national staff, if not the local one. The audience received the national director cooly, for there had been conflict between Chattanooga and the national office. Even though Chattanooga was recognized as one of the best programs, Excel enthusiasts there too had tried to put some distance between themselves and the national office.

At the end of the meeting everyone sang, "Let Us Plan Together," a song composed by one of the local teachers. Whatever the effect on the students, the Chattanooga program was clearly a boost to teacher morale, with much feeling, enthusiasm, and commitment from the audience, which was overwhelmingly black.

Grass-roots Origins

The Chattanooga program had been initiated by Johnny Holloway, an engineer and vice president of the local chapter of the National Association for the Advancement of Colored People. Holloway had the reputation of being a "careful" activist, a commanding speaker, and a power within any organization to which he belonged. In 1977 Holloway tried out the Excel principles with his own children, and he was so impressed with the results that he started a petition to introduce Excel into the Chattanooga schools. The petition was signed by 4,000 people, and the school district agreed to establish a program in October 1977 (S. Murray and C. Murray 1980).

The national coordinator of PUSH, William Thurston, was invited to speak to the Chattanooga Chamber of Commerce, and both the Chattanooga superintendent of schools and the Tennessee commissioner of education endorsed the program. Plans were made to introduce the program into six schools, beginning with Howard High School, and an agreement was drawn up between the Chattanooga schools and PUSH for Excellence. In March 1978 the Chamber of Commerce endorsed Excel, and in April Jesse Jackson was invited to address a community benefit, his trip paid for by the Chamber of Commerce.

The structure of the local organization was similar to that of the Denver program, at least superficially. The director and community liaisons were subject to the authority of the national office, and the district coordinator and teacher-advisors were formally accountable to the school district. A governing staff consisting of parents, teachers, students, and community representatives oversaw the program in each school. The governing enterprise worked much better in Chattanooga than in Denver, however.

The district Advisory Committee served as an overall steering committee, providing strong direction and actually dismissing personnel when necessary. It effectively integrated the local PUSH structure, the schools, and the community. When it took action, the action was concerted and authoritative. The key to this success was the composition of the Committee. Included on the first Advisory Committee were the superintendent of schools, the assistant superintendent of schools, a key minister, Johnny Holloway, and other important community figures. The Committee eventually included some of the most powerful people in Chattanooga as well as the top officials in the school system and the principals in whose schools the program operated. Once agreement was reached about how to proceed, the Advisory Committee was in a strong position to influence the program.

The person who seemed to exert the most direct influence was Clifford Hendrix, the assistant superintendent of the Chattanooga Schools and the highest-ranking black in the school district. Hendrix seemed highly competent, simultaneously committed to making the program work and sensitive to the Chattanooga power structure. Because of his administrative position he had direct control of school personnel, and on the Advisory Committee he could influence how other power figures perceived the program. He put his full authority behind PUSH/Excel and was a central figure in making the program work.

The Power Structure

Chattanooga did not have the same kind of power structure as did Chicago, Los Angeles, Denver, or Kansas City. Local citizens agreed in various interviews that ten families virtually ran the city. Those families lived on Lookout Mountain, and nothing happened without their approval. The power structure of Chattanooga was more hierarchical, narrow, and monolithic than in the big cities of the north and west. Once these families decided that PUSH/Excel would be tried, it was given a fair chance. Without their endorsement, PUSH/Excel would never have gotten off the ground, according to several knowledgeable sources.

The key figure in the community was Ruth S. Holmberg, publisher of the *Chattanooga Times* and related to the Sulzberger family of the *New York Times*. Holmberg accepted PUSH/Excel as a cause and convinced other members of the establishment to support it. Eventually she became chair of the Advisory Committee, a position that gave her the opportunity to do the program many good turns. When Jackson made his highly publicized trip to the Middle East in 1979, it did not have the same repercussions in Chattanooga as it did elsewhere. Although Holmberg was concerned, Jackson made a special visit to the city to placate her, and she continued her strong support for the program. The Middle East trip was not emphasized in her newspaper as much as elsewhere. In fact, the Jewish population of Chattanooga was relatively small and nonvocal compared to those of other PUSH/Excel cities.

Nor did Jackson acquire the negative image in Chattanooga that he did elsewhere. Even a member of the Chamber of Commerce, which had financed Jackson's first trip to the city, said there was no problem with Jackson's Middle East stance. The local people understood that there was not necessarily a direct connection between the local and national operations. Jackson was great at stirring things up, but Chattanoogans knew he was volatile and would be on to something else next week. Although the Excel program would not have started without him, they all agreed that Chattanooga was on its own.

By 1981 the Advisory Committee had been expanded to twenty-eight members, including principals, parents, a bank president, an attorney, a corporate executive, and at Jackson's suggestion, local disc jockeys. Faced by the threat of withdrawal of federal funds, the Committee concentrated on fund-raising. More than 50 percent of the program costs came from local donations, while the school district and federal government each provided 25 percent. The Lindhurst Foundation had already put $70,000 into the program before the AIR evaluation was released, but the other two large local foundations had not yet contributed. The negative evaluation report produced by AIR seriously hurt the fund-raising efforts.

Of course, the central power structure in this southern city was white, but the Baptist church played an important role in the black community. As Jackson had experienced in his childhood, the black preacher was attributed great authority and high esteem. Black ministers were prominent at the retreat on Lookout Mountain and made frequent comments about the various issues that were raised. The black community was integrated into the community through its churches, no doubt in a subordinate manner, but integrated nonetheless. The school, the church, and the family were the cornerstones of the Chattanooga program, much as Jackson had envisioned.

Unlike Denver, Chattanooga had solved the riddle of a dual organizational structure through the authority of the Advisory Committee, which had successfully integrated not only PUSH and the schools but also the community powers. This concentrated power was unlike the pluralistic power structure of the other cities, and of course the school district was committed to making the program work. And it did work better in Chattanooga than in any other city.

Judging the Choir

The schools chosen for the Chattanooga program were the three with the most serious problems. On the one hand, Hendrix, the assistant superintendent, was concerned about the leadership within the schools. The assistant principal in each school was supposed to take the lead in managing the program, but only one was actually doing so. On the other hand, the community support and the PUSH/Excel staff worked well. Initially, some PUSH staff members didn't know how to work with parents, teachers, and students, according to Hendrix, but these staffers were then replaced. The staff advisors were selected by the principals, as in Denver, and the advisors appeared to be highly committed to the program, even though they might be an assistant principal, a counselor, or a dean of students, and not full-time with the program. Each year the governance committee for each school chose a focus for the year, such as absenteeism or tardiness, and the teacher-advisors and the community liaisons then coordinated activities (Hendrix 1981).

During the first year of the program there were problems with regard to the community liaisons. They were not formally trained, and they felt their role was neither understood nor appreciated by the professional school personnel. The principals and teachers thought the work hours of the liaisons were too lax (Gee 1981). The community liaisons, on the other hand, claimed they needed flexibility to work in the community at unusual hours (Caldwell 1981). To resolve these differences, the liaisons were scheduled to spend from 11 A.M. to 3 P.M. in the school and from 3 P.M. to 7 P.M. in the community. In-school activities were mostly motivational, and community activities were aimed at involving parents— the most difficult aspect of the program.

One inventive activity was the grandparents project. Even when meetings were arranged with parents to talk about their children's problems, the chances of the parents showing up were not always good. Howard High School countered this problem by involving the grandparents. The grandparents would make appointments for the parents, and if the parents did not show up, the grandparents were likely to call them up and redress them. As a result the percentage of involved parents increased dramatically—a comment on the status of elders in the black community.

At another school, a dinner was given for students who were chronic absentees and their parents. The staff invited a local disc jockey, who tried to find out why the students skipped school. Activities at other schools included pledge drives, assemblies, chapel programs, awards and incentives, report card pickups, and media campaigns. In addition, there were parent volunteers, tutorials, and a PUSH/Excel choir. Special events included a career fair, an open house, a school visitation night, a convocation, PUSH/Excel week, and a teacher orientation (S. Murray et al. 1982).

Volunteers from senior citizens groups and tutors from the Baptist church participated. Ministers provided counseling at schools, and parents offered their homes for PUSH/Excel parties. Businesses made financial contributions, and in other schools there were essay contests, Black History month, visits to colleges, guest speakers, voter registration drives, newsletters, drawing contests, beauty contests, parades, business workshops, buddy systems, parent rallies, film presentations, dances, and attendance parties.

When the principals first heard about the program, they had been reluctant to become involved because they expected that support for the program would eventually disappear, as had most federally supported efforts. The attendance problems were so desperate, however, that they were willing to give the program a chance. Malcolm Walker, the district coordinator, had worked well with the local schools in the past, and most local newspaper reports about the program had been favorable (Gee 1981).

The relationship between Chattanooga and the national office was always a strained one, as in fact it had been with most of the local programs. The Lindhurst Foundation offer of a $75,000 grant over a period of three years was contingent upon evidence of community involvement, particularly a "stage concert with the audience paying admission." The national office offered to arrange for the concert through Jackson's personal contacts with big-name entertainers, but nothing came of the promise, and although the Lindhurst grant was awarded, the Chattanoogans did not forget that the national office had not followed through on its word. Walker, the district coordinator, raised the issue publicly at an Advisory Committee meeting attended by Elma Mardis, the national director. She became angry and afterward was barely on speaking terms with Walker. By 1981 Walker and others felt that the national office had little to offer them. Even though the Chattanooga contract with Operation PUSH specified that the national office was to provide technical assistance to Chattanooga, Walker thought Chattanooga should be providing technical assistance to the national office instead (Walker 1981).

Wendall Morgan, the second local director, and his staff were more positive about the national office. Jackson was still an inspirational figure to the students as well as to the teachers. The students memorized Jackson's thoughts and sayings and were enthusiastic about them. How the students responded was the real test of the program, in Morgan's view. The national evaluation may have reported negative results, but as a school liaison said, "You can't judge a choir by statistics" (Caldwell 1981). Enthusiasm was what counted. The very presence of the program made students and staff feel that somebody cared about them, that they were important.

All in all, the PUSH/Excel program in Chattanooga seemed to work better than any of the other federally supported demonstration sites. Although there were problems, there was also staff dedication and support, and the power structure tried to make it work. This community effort was partly due to the fact that Chattanooga was a southern community very much like the one Jackson had grown up in. The program fit the community better than in the other cities. And although Chattanooga was quiet on the surface, there were racial tensions underneath[2]—perhaps this tension was one reason the power establishment was so supportive of the program, though no one said this directly.

Nonetheless, the program seemed to be working there and was gathering momentum. It was not killed by desegregation politics, as in Chicago or Los Angeles. Nor was it killed by ethnic politics, as in Denver, Memphis, and New Orleans. It was finally wounded by the national evaluation. On March 23, 1982, key members of the Chattanooga Advisory Committee met with AIR evaluator Saundra Murray to discuss the contents of the final evaluation report. The meeting was stormy, as the Chattanooga people argued that the report totally misrepresented the Chattanooga program. Their ire was most forcefully expressed by Jane Harbaugh, who said to Murray, "What you have done is really killed us all."

Notes

1. A former teacher and member of an advisory board, John Bates, thought the real problem resided with the teachers. There was a lack of commitment on their part, and the teachers were not really available to the students. When he had taught before his retirement, he had known the students' backgrounds and visited their homes. Now teachers were commuters, not even living in the same neighborhoods as the students, he said. They neither knew about the students nor cared. This problem was not something that teacher-advisors or community liaisons could solve for the teachers; they had to do it for themselves. Instead, he said, teachers blamed the parents, but the parents were trying to maintain their families through low-paying jobs and difficult livelihoods that did not permit them to come to school for planning periods. Teacher involvement had to start from the central office, from the administration, but there had never been enough administrative support or pressure on the teachers to participate, in his opinion. Bates was raised in the South and he strongly concurred with Jackson's notion that moral authority was secured by having the school on one side, the parents on another, and the church on the third side, with the students

in the middle. That was the kind of authority necessary to make any real difference (Bates 1981).

2. An example: When black community leaders wanted to change the name of a street to Martin Luther King Plaza, a man planning to construct a building on the street said he would not do so if the name was changed. Eventually, only the lower part of the street, lined with used car dealers and pawn shops, was renamed. And there were racial outbursts after four black women were shot on the street by members of the Ku Klux Klan in 1980.

6

The Federal Evaluation

As the program developed at local sites around the country, the National Institute of Education (NIE) planned the evaluation of PUSH/ Excel. Norman Gold, senior research associate, was responsible for drafting the Request for Proposal (RFP) for the evaluation competition.[1] Gold cast the evaluation RFP in broad terms, giving potential bidders considerable latitude for its design.

The RFP noted that the evaluation had a variety of potential audiences—parents, teachers, community members, policy makers and evaluators—and that the evaluation contractor would consult with panels representative of the different "user" groups. In particular, the RFP stated that "What [users] need to know and when they need to have information from the evaluation will be important in informing the development of the design" and noted at the same time that this approach did not imply a "technical compromise" that would "satisfy consumers but not stand up to a review of methodological rigor and clarity" (National Institute of Education 1978). The work was to be conducted in two phases, with four months to design the evaluation and thirty-two months to carry it out. The first phase was to familiarize the contractor with the program and provide information on what the prospective audiences would expect from the evaluation. The evaluation's usefulness would be enhanced if the information needs of the audience were reflected in the final design (Gold 1981). Gold and his colleagues later conscientiously funded a study of this "stakeholder" approach itself.[2]

The evaluation contract process advanced swiftly. The RFP was released in September 1978; proposals were due in October; and the contract was signed in January 1979, with a budget of $750,000. NIE received seven proposals in the competition, which Gold described as "not a hot competition. The proposals weren't great." The contract was awarded "reluctantly" to the American Institutes for Research (AIR), a well-respected private contract research group located in the Georgetown area of Washington, D.C., despite Gold's uneasiness that AIR was "relying too much on Charlie Murray," who was conducting a similar evaluation of another educational program. AIR won the contract because, in Gold's words, "We knew they understood what the stakeholder concept was all about" (Gold 1980a).

"Investment Behaviors"

AIR staff members had been involved in several overseas projects funded by the Agency for International Development and considered themselves to be experts in the "problems of disadvantages." Specifically, they had been part of a "massive rural development effort to strengthen Thailand against the domino theory" (American Institutes for Research 1980, 3). They had developed assessment techniques for over thirty interventions, or rural development programs, and Paul Schwarz, president of AIR, had once been director of AIR's international operations.

The principal investigator for the PUSH/Excel evaluation and author of the proposal was Charles Murray, who had worked in Thailand in the late 1960s and early 1970s, and whose doctoral dissertation had been on investment and tithing in Thai villages. In the mid-1970s he had participated in U.S. criminal justice studies and had become involved in particular in various studies dealing with juvenile offenders. He was appointed project director of AIR's Cities-in-Schools evaluation and named "chief scientist" for AIR's Washington office in 1975. This position made him responsible for the technical quality of all AIR reports and involved him in preparing proposals for new projects. Within a few years, Murray won three large contracts worth a total of $5.1 million, including the evaluation of PUSH/Excel.

Later, in 1984, Murray was to become well known for his book *Losing Ground* (Murray 1984), which developed the thesis that the social programs and policies of the 1960s had actually damaged their poor black recipients because the benefits made them unwilling and unable to work. Murray's book originated as a paper for the conservative Heritage Foundation, and he was funded to write the book by the Manhattan Institute, another conservative think tank, with intellectual sponsorship from Irving Kristol, founding father of the neoconservatives. Murray's book became front-page news in the mid-1980s and the Reagan Republicans often cited it in their attacks on social programs. Those developments in Murray's career were in the future, however, when Murray designed the evaluation of PUSH/Excel in 1979.

An important addition to the AIR staff was Saundra R. Murray (no relation to the principal investigator, Charles Murray). Saundra Murray

the evaluators made the motivation for improvement seem primarily economic. Financial rewards were certainly an important part of the conservative black capitalism that Jackson preached—but so were black pride, morality, and authority, which are not primarily economic in nature. The investment motif on which the evaluation was based missed the source of the motivational wellspring of PUSH/Excel. Second, to cast PUSH/Excel into the industrial production metaphor, focusing on inputs and outputs and looking for mechanical and machine-like functions, misconstrued the symbolic nature of the program itself. The evaluators expected the program to be analyzable and reducible to standard components that could be plugged into different settings. PUSH/Excel, with its religious type of fervor and symbolic forms, was nothing like a machine or an assembly line with uniform components, as the evaluators were to discover only too late. The evaluators, proceeding logically from their artificial framework, developed an evaluation plan that presumed a program very different from the actual symbolic, religious, motivational program they were evaluating.

At one point, though, they did caution themselves: "The evaluation must recognize that PUSH/Excel has a route to impact that bypasses all of the usual trappings of a social action program: impact can occur simply because someone has listened to the Rev. Jackson's speeches and has been motivated to act" (S. Murray and C. Murray 1979, 8). Unfortunately they did not attend to their own cautions. The evaluation they had so conscientiously designed was highly likely to show PUSH/Excel in a bad light, given the lack of standardization that characterized the program from the beginning. Neither was there much attention in the final design to the stakeholder concept that had been one of the original goals of the evaluation.

Reactions to the Design

A draft of the evaluation design was ready in time for the annual PUSH/Excel national convention, held in Cleveland May 29–31, 1979, but it was not distributed until two days after Saundra Murray had reviewed it with Excel national and local personnel. AIR noted that because the oral briefing had taken place before the design was made available, "it could not be expected that specific suggestions for revision would be forthcoming" (S. Murray and N. Thompkins 1979). However, PUSH/Excel staff did express two concerns at the briefing: what AIR meant by wanting to be "helpful" to the program and what their statement about ensuring "the independence of the evaluation from external influence" meant (p. 14). Norman Gold handled the second issue by noting that safeguards ensured that the PUSH/Excel staff itself would pass on the "fairness and validity" of the evaluation but also that AIR independence would be protected—a serious contradiction, in my view. Few other questions arose about the design, because, in Saundra Murray's view:

> At that point, the evaluation had very low visibility. James Comer at Yale was doing an evaluation that was *their* evaluation, and there was only a minimum of interest in what we were doing. [Attention was on Comer] because he has status in the black community, lots of status. He wrote *Black Child Care* with Al Poussaint, who is on the PUSH/Excel board. They both have very high visibility in the black community. He also writes a syndicated column on child care which appears in black newspapers. Their names were practically household words, and they had major visibility, which we lacked (S. Murray 1980).

A month later, Charles Warfield, PUSH director of operations, met with the AIR evaluation team to express two more concerns. First, he said that Excel was a social action program whose impact might occur independently of local program activities and that consequently AIR should study social movement effects; second, that the evaluation should take political issues into account because they were affecting local implementation. AIR also received a letter from Cordell Richardson, Excel western regional director, who was "generally pleased about [the] suggested approach and the accompanying rationale." He had not yet discussed the design with other national Excel staff but said he would express any concern to AIR at the "appropriate time."

NIE called the evaluators to a formal meeting about the design in mid-July. Three members of a Technical Advisory Panel hired by NIE to review the design also attended this meeting: Dr. Peter Rossi, director of the Social and Demographic Research Institute at the University of Massachusetts; Dr. Paul M. Wortman, codirector of the Psychology Department's Methodology and Evaluation Research group at Northwestern University; and Dr. Edgar Epps of the University of Chicago. This panel expressed fundamental concerns about the evaluation in written reviews to NIE. From Wortman:

> In all candor, my first reaction is that it is impossible and unfeasible to evaluate PUSH/Excel at this time. Quite simply there is no program yet evident. In our discussions, P/E was variously referred to as "a philosophy," a "social-action movement," a "thing," and a "schmear." The program is still ill-formed and ill-defined with very little in the way of concrete tangible elements. This has left the evaluation staff groping about looking for something to grab onto. They have finally come up with four goals which may be best described as states of mind or in psychological lingo intervening variables.

As their evaluation plan acknowledges, these goals still must be translated into concrete program activity. In the meantime though, one must ask is there a program to evaluate (Wortman 1979).

Rossi's reaction was in a similar vein:

> Finally, I must admit to being baffled by the description of PUSH/Excel as developed during the meetings. On the one hand I am very much influenced by those of you [who] have been exposed to the Reverend Jackson and by how deeply impressed you have been by his charismatic ability. Charisma is a necessary but embarrassing concept in sociology. On the other hand, I am also impressed by the fact that the PUSH/Excel movement is improvising its activities as it goes along and hence is amateurish and lacking in technical expertise. Whether the charisma is more than a transitory influence and can overcome the hit and miss improvisation is a serious question (Rossi 1979).

Epps did not submit a written review. The evaluation design eventually received qualified approval from the national PUSH/Excel staff, the federal staff, and the Technical Advisory Panel. Reservations were expressed about whether and how to evaluate Excel, but because the assessment had to be done, these reservations were put aside in the interest of making the evaluation technically sound and useful for program development. For their part, Gold and his federal colleagues liked AIR's emphasis on documenting activities. They agreed with AIR that Excel was fragmented and disorganized by most program standards and concluded that the program was still in the early stages of development. But they thought that the PUSH staff needed technical feedback in order to develop it further. AIR's incremental evaluation approach seemed particularly well suited for this purpose, they thought.

The technical advisors were more cautious about the nature of Excel: They fussed over the question of what to call it and how to characterize it, skeptical that Excel could be evaluated. Not surprisingly, they were also at a loss to suggest how to evaluate something that they thought was not yet a program and might never be one, given their view of what a program was. But they did recommend various evaluation design improvements. Warfield's suggestion that Jackson's movement might have effects independent of local activities was not heeded; no one knew how to respond to the suggestion. AIR, NIE, and the technical experts thought they knew how to evaluate more conventional programs, but not movements or crusades. They finally agreed that Excel was a "program-in-development," and that AIR's incremental approach would provide the guidance that PUSH/Excel needed. The evaluation proceeded.

The Technocratic View

All the talk about whether PUSH/Excel was a program or only a movement hinted at the eventual findings of the evaluation. With their notion of the industrial production metaphor for social programs, the evaluators had particular expectations about what a program should be and could be. These implicit expectations became quite explicit in the negative judgments they eventually rendered about PUSH/Excel in the evaluation reports. In their view a coherent program was a coordinated, sequential set of standard activities, with each activity tied to specific outcomes and each activity repeated and sustained. The program had to be specified by detailed, step-by-step concrete procedures and justified by an explicit strategy and rationale. Moreover, the program had to be guided and monitored by a central authority that would provide a how-to manual for participants. They thought that this central authority should conduct its own internal evaluation and maintain firm management of local sites, and that activities and results should recur across sites.

In fact, the PUSH/Excel program did not fit this image at all. It could not meet these rigid standards of what a social program should be, nor, quite frankly, could most social programs; nor could the universities the technical experts came from, the federal government, or probably AIR itself meet these standards. PUSH/Excel could not even come close, and as a result would be declared a failure on every single count. But the failure was partly due to the mismatch between the the evaluators' conception of the program and the PUSH/Excel concept. If it was a "program" at all, PUSH/Excel was a symbolic, religious, motivational program, more like what Baptist ministers mean when they say they have a "program" for their church. It was emotional, voluntaristic, and symbolic. It was decentralized; there were few standard, uniform activities across all sites. Program activities were local, opportunistic, and adventitious, and were often "one-shot" events. The evaluators' conceptual scheme could not accommodate this type of program. Their framework was predicated upon the notion that there were discrete, standard, uniform activities, clearly definable, which would routinely result in specified behaviors. If such uniform activities and results did not exist, they could not evaluate the program. Their conceptual scheme was inflexible in this regard, and so PUSH/Excel was stretched upon this blueprint. It was expected to resemble a highly articulated machine or assembly line, complete with components, modules, and products.

This technocratic view of the social world as a machine, as assembly line, as industrial production, was entirely foreign to Jesse Jackson's view of the world and of how the world could be changed—in fact, of how it was possible to change the world. Charisma, emotion, and conversion had no place in this technocratic vision. The only way to deal with such ideas was to declare that they did not exist or that they did not count. Based upon their conceptual framework, the evaluators would declare logically that there was no program; at the same time they witnessed with their own eyes mass conversions and numerous activities that motivated people to action. Their training in social science had taught them to see certain things other people could not see; it had also taught them *not* to see things that others could see. To their credit, at one point the AIR evaluators asked, with the blessing of AIR management, that the evaluation be discontinued, that it be held in abeyance. They were disturbed at the mismatch between their conceptual framework and that of PUSH/Excel (C. Murray 1982a; Schwarz 1982). But the entire endeavor was far too enmeshed in the bureaucratic machinery, the politics of the situation, and the mass media, to disengage. The evaluation proceeded.

For their part, Jesse Jackson and the PUSH/Excel staff never seemed to understand what the problem was nor to anticipate that they were likely to have difficulties with the evaluation. They would eventually condemn the negative evaluation findings as politically motivated. Their own thinking was far too removed from the technocratic mentality to comprehend the problem.

Notes

1. Gold had joined NIE in 1973 from the Office of Economic Opportunity, where he was director of evaluation for community action and program development.

2. See Stake 1986 for the development of the "stakeholder" concept within the National Institute of Education.

3. See House 1983 for an explication of this general metaphoric framework and the use of metaphors in evaluation.

4. The evaluators hoped to document the results for each small sequence of steps that they hypothesized in the rationale. Sometimes these specifications became quite detailed. For example, for student pledges evaluators would document how each activity led to each outcome by collecting data on adjacent events (S. Murray and C. Murray 1979, 19). After the student signed the pledge, the evaluators hypothesized that only certain results could follow. The evaluators would document the signing of the pledge at each site; after documenting what happened after the pledge signings, the evaluators would be able to determine how the pledges affected student motivation. With these statistics, the evaluators would then have felt they had discovered a cause-and-effect segment, a "knowledge module." The basic cause-and-effect relationships would be "validated" by observing them across several sites.

These "knowledge modules" would then be accumulated and fed back to program developers for possible modification. Adjacent events would be linked to each other, and the evaluation would become a series of "go" and "no-go" decisions. Only if the prior link had been established would resources be devoted to the next link. Thus, the evaluation would focus on short-term activities and outcomes, cause-and-effect relationships. Of course, the success of this approach depended on the evaluators' being able to specify a particular sequence of uniform events—which they could not, as it turned out.

5. In the final design of the evaluation, AIR's evaluators developed their own rationale for the program and charted it in diagrams. According to their rationale the national and local PUSH/Excel program efforts would lead to parent, school, and community involvement, which would lead in turn to student involvement, attitude shifts, and practice investments. Student involvement, in turn, would result in increased motivation, responsibility, better school atmosphere, and more opportunity. These outcomes would lead to "investments," defined as "voluntary expenditures of time, effort, or money, to pursue legitimate opportunities in hopes of a future return" (S. Murray and C. Murray 1979, 10). Finally, these personal investments would result in improved achievement.

Using PUSH/Excel documents and their own definitions of terms, the evaluators designated student achievement as the most distant outcome, with student investment, motivation, responsibility, school atmosphere, and student opportunity as necessary prerequisites to student achievement. The subgoals would be affected in turn by student, parent, and community involvement and "practice investments."

This basic rationale enabled the evaluators to select indicators of change. For each of these subgoals or components, the evaluators would collect quantitative indicators, usually scales rating student attitudes. Both the causal sequences and measures of outcomes would be selected by reference to the basic rationale. The *Evaluation Design* listed many measures of parent, community, and school outcomes, most of which would be collected through interviews. Measures of impact and investment would be collected from students. Yet other indicators, such as attendance, could be gleaned from school records. Part-time on-site observers would record local PUSH/Excel activities as they occurred. These observed activities would then be linked to the outcomes to establish "knowledge modules," which could be tested across sites to see if the same results occurred elsewhere. Such was the basic evaluation design.

7

The Federal Verdict:
No Program

The months immediately following the NIE's approval of the evaluation design were busy ones for AIR. Plans called for parent and student interviews in the fall of 1979, a step that first involved obtaining federal approval of the questionnaires AIR planned to administer on local sites. NIE had hoped to arrange for a speedy forms clearance, a required procedure on federal projects, but months passed, through no fault on the part of AIR, before approval was finally granted in December 1979, two years and four months after the programs had started at the older sites, and four months after they had started in the three new ones—Memphis, Denver, and Chattanooga. AIR's design now called for collecting their "predata" from sites that already had been in operation for some time.

The First Evaluation Report, March 1980

AIR's first evaluation report, *The National Evaluation of the PUSH for Excellence Project: Technical Report 1: The Evolution of a Program* (S. Murray and C. Murray 1980), displayed tables of activities in which parents, community, school staff, and students had participated. These lists of activities were extensive, with different local sites sponsoring different activities. For example, Chattonooga held ten different school assemblies during the fall of 1979 and a similar number of activities in the community. Chattanooga also sponsored three student activities that were the same for all participating schools plus two to five other student activities that differed for each school. In contrast, there were only two teacher activities in Chattanooga. Throughout the evaluation AIR did a commendable job of describing these activities; however, in spite of this considerable amount of PUSH/Excel activity, the evaluators did not think these efforts constituted proper program development. The main substance of their report focused on the inadequacy of the activities:

> By the end of fall 1979, PUSH/Excel in the six cities comprised one-time events (e.g., convocations, community rallies, and meetings) and a diverse set of ongoing activities that engaged small groups of participants. Sustained sequences of activities at the school level . . . were virtually absent.
>
> The current standard for involvement is that there should be activities for each element: parents, communities, schools and the students. By that standard, none of the sites is fully implemented at the school level. . . . In short, a coherent program of total involvement has not evolved (S. Murray and C. Murray 1980, 40).

AIR attributed this lack of a "coherent program" to the emphasis on promotion at the national office: "National has focused more on program promotion and expansion than on sustained efforts toward elaborating the involvement concept to make it work. Formal guidelines for implementing PUSH/Excel are yet to appear" (p. 42). In this first report AIR struck a theme that would continue throughout the evaluation: According to AIR's definition, PUSH/Excel had no program. It had no coordinated group of activities tied to measurable outcomes, no step-by-step description, no how-to manual. Although the first evaluation report listed pages of activities, these were one-time events with little follow-up and minimal guidance from the national office. There were no directives, no internal evaluation, and no central office monitoring.

The press was particularly interested in AIR's report. For several months before its publication, Spencer Rich, staff writer for the *Washington Post*, had been regularly phoning AIR and NIE for a copy. When it was finally available, Rich wrote a front-page story that appeared April 22, 1980. Entitled "U.S. Study Faults Jesse Jackson's School Program," the article said, "Despite $2 million in federal appropriations voted so far and an additional $1 million likely, the Reverend Jesse Jackson has failed to convert the high ideals and inspirational message of his PUSH/Excel movement into a systematic, workable, public school program, according to a new government report." The *Post* story portrayed a charismatic leader who was long on rhetoric to promote his program but who had failed to follow up with a program that worked. The story emphasized the lack of programmatic activities, monitoring, and strong management by the national office. AIR knew specifically what it meant when it said "no coherent program," but "no program" in the context of the *Post* article implied something else—malfeasance and possibly worse.

The uncomplimentary *Post* article was disseminated widely through the wire services; it produced many calls to NIE and AIR and eight radio interviews for Saundra Murray and Charles Murray. Saundra Murray attributed some of this attention to the Washington Youth March for Summer Jobs that Jackson was trying to organize. In the view of one national Excel staffer, the march subsequently failed because of the negative publicity generated by the first evaluation report.

Jackson and his legal staff were "appalled at the findings." Why? "Because we said they weren't a program, but a movement. Jackson said that that was a slap in the face to the civil rights movement. *That* was a movement, and it was sacred, and you couldn't put PUSH/Excel in that league," Saundra Murray said (1980). But she disagreed. Excel was exactly like a movement, she thought.

> In fact, the PUSH/Excel staff had referred to it as a movement themselves. But I think that Jesse has taken on the mantle of Martin Luther King. He speaks of him a lot and seems to see himself as his successor. And someone on the [Technical Advisory Panel] said that this evaluation could be the end of the civil rights movement if Jesse's stature is diminished. People don't want to see Jesse hurt, and a negative evaluation will hurt him personally. Lots of people love him, and he keeps poor black people in the public eye. They don't want him to lose his stature and his reputation (S. Murray 1980).

Murray thought the national staff considered the report negative because "we thought the management was lousy, and that it wasn't a program but a movement. But I think it never would have come up if Jackson had not gone to the Middle East."

A major confrontation between the PUSH/Excel supporters and Saundra Murray occurred that summer at the annual Operation PUSH convention; this confrontation left Murray sorely conflicted and "torn up" about the evaluation. First, Murray gave a speech, which AIR Vice President Victor Rouse told her was "cruel" because she told her audience:

> A lot of flashy activities do not amount to a product. A lot of people running these programs are amateurs and don't know what they're doing and aren't getting any honest feedback. For the first three years that Excel was in existence, they got away for hell. The funders didn't shoot straight about what was going on, and they didn't force the people to shape up. They need honest feedback and I plan to give it to them (S. Murray 1980).

Next Murray was scheduled to participate in a plenary session to discuss the Allan Bakke reverse discrimination case. She thought her inclusion on that panel somewhat odd but agreed in the interest of giving the AIR study visibility. Hours before the panel was to convene, the topic was switched from Bakke to "PUSH/Excel, Success or Failure." On stage with Murray were Jesse Jackson himself, Mary Frances Berry,

James Comer, and Al Poussaint. The panel was billed as a major conference event, and the hall was filled: "All the people who mattered were there," Murray said. The following ensued, as Murray reported later in an interview:

> Comer said that the evaluation was "excessively visible." Berry said that they had "hoped for a sensitive evaluation." Then [I] got up and said that AIR was using the most sophisticated evaluation methodology available. . . . PUSH/Excel wanted to develop a program, but interest and energy were beginning to wane in the sites. [I] concluded by hoping that the evaluation would be useful to the sites but that it was up to the national [office] to revitalize the organization (S. Murray 1980).

Saundra Murray said she was later told that the panel was "a set up." She was seen as the enemy and the panel had been designed to embarrass AIR and discredit the evaluation. She didn't think the ploy succeeded, but the reactions to *Technical Report 1* took a toll on her. She reported feeling "wiped out and burned out." Murray talked about personal conflicts that the evaluation stirred up for her and how it affected her personal and professional goals:

> Blacks said to me, "How could you do this to another black person?" We need to help kids, but we need to take blacks seriously, not just throw money at them. No one ever values [black] products. We can get money, plenty of money, because blacks are in, but it has nothing to do with what we do or whether its quality is high (S. Murray 1980).

Press interest in Excel's evaluation catapulted AIR's gloomy findings into major news stories and shaped public opinion about the program. Whereas the media had previously been a strong force in rallying public support for Jackson's movement, it now announced that Excel had not lived up to its promise. The theme of "no program" was converted into a theme of program failure and perhaps irresponsibility. The stereotype whites often held of black leaders enhanced this theme. Saundra Murray said the report was misunderstood by the media, but her comments were to no avail. Even though PUSH/Excel tried to counter with its own media message, it was never able to escape this negative judgment.

Although the PUSH/Excel national staff argued publicly with AIR's first technical report, privately they agreed that something had to be done about the program. They were in trouble with the media and with the local program staffs, who felt that the national office did little to help them and that Jackson's unrelated political activities only made local problems worse (Farrar 1980; Gold 1980, 1982; S. Murray 1980).

In response to these criticisms, a PUSH/Excel Implementation Task Force was convened shortly after the report appeared. It included Elma Mardis, the new national director; her staff assistant, Maurice Sykes; the Chattanooga Excel director; Norman Gold; Saundra Murray; and Kathlyn Moses, program officer for Excel in the Department of Education. Their task was to develop an "implementation guide" for local staff. National Excel personnel and federal officials had approved of the program rationale developed by AIR. Mardis and her staff agreed to take the first crack at developing a handbook for Excel implementation, using the evaluators' rationale as a framework.

Later the national office also contracted with the Center for New Schools, a private organization, to develop a PUSH/Excel implementation guide. This decision was pressed on the national office by federal officials and AIR, and it signaled PUSH/Excel's acquiescence to the federal view that the program needed more systematic development: If the program was not producing the effects that the evaluation tried to find, perhaps a more structured approach to achieving those effects would be successful. Under pressure, the PUSH/Excel staff accepted the evaluators' views as to how the program should develop.

The Second Evaluation Report, September 1980

Data collection and analysis proceeded through the spring and summer, and *The National Evaluation of the PUSH for Excellence Project: Technical Report 2: Implementation* (S. Murray et al. 1980) was submitted to NIE in September. It was billed as an "update, not a full-fledged evaluation of the first year's program" (p. 3). During the intervening six months, the Los Angeles program had lost the support of the school district and Memphis had abandoned plans to begin. Thus the second report, narrower in scope than the first, dealt with only Chicago, Chattanooga, and Denver. It focused on the past year's activities at each site and presented an elaborated rationale for Excel's future.

This second report was somewhat more positive than the first. It noted that the "sites are building systematically" (p. 37) and that there was now an *Implementation Guide* to instruct local sites. The guide itself had adopted the sequential rationale of the evaluators and suggested that there were two phases of implementation—transition and prein-vestment—into which all PUSH/Excel activities could be sorted. The Excel people were using the language and concepts of the evaluators, and the evaluators applauded this improvement, noting that "For each outcome there is at least one site with an activity that could plausibly lead to an expected end" (p. 48). Less positively, they noted that most of the activities fell into the first phase of transition rather than the second of preinvestment.

The balance of the report dealt with development activities, specifically with the local efforts to detail the paths linking activities to the expected outcomes. It noted that the Chicago program staffers had not done much of this kind of development, while Chattanooga and Denver were making progress. But it also noted that because programs were developing differently at the three sites, the early "success indicators" would be quite different in each city. Furthermore, the recent program development efforts spelled out in the new *Implementation Guide* did not completely reflect what was actually happening at the sites. This discrepancy, it said, had created problems for the evaluators, who had hoped to use the new program rationale as the official model against which to assess program progress.

The upshot was that the local sites were urged to get on track with the new program model. Until they did so, or until a new site got under way using the official program plan from the start, the evaluators could not proceed as planned. They could document progress but could not do a thorough evaluation because the program had not yet reached the point where it was providing the inputs whose outcomes AIR could assess. More precisely, "PUSH/Excel in 1979-1980 did not constitute a 'program' as that term is usually meant" (p. 77). Activities were too episodic and unsettled, and development was occurring only in fits and starts.

In concluding, AIR observed that Excel had made real progress toward developing a concrete program and implementation plan. Nonetheless, much depended on the political and technical skills of local staff to execute the plans. As local progress—or the lack of it—had implications for the evaluation, AIR recommended continuing the evaluation at a lower level of effort through the 1980-1981 school year. By then, it would be clear whether an "evaluable program has been put in place" (p. 83).

Technical Report 2 was submitted to NIE in September 1980, and this time NIE anticipated problems with the press. In an interview in 1980, Charles Murray reported what ensued:

> The way [NIE] treated that second report, you would have thought they had a time bomb in their hands. [*Post* reporter] Spencer Rich had known after the first report when the second was coming out, and he started phoning into NIE as soon as that date arrived, and kept being put off legitimately, kept being told the draft had not been given to NIE yet. And then when we were finally ready with one . . . [NIE] convened a meeting in the secretary or deputy secretary's office, and we were all sitting around trying to decide

whether to keep this confidential and make the *Post* sue under the Freedom of Information Act, and they wanted us to number all the [review] copies to ensure that it didn't leak.

I know Norman [Gold] took the line that [not releasing it] undercut the stakeholder process, that we had a clearly defined review process that he did not want to compromise. I guarantee you that the compromise of the stakeholder review process is not the reason for the meeting in the secretary's office and the rest of that. They were scared of Jesse. They wanted to cover their ass. They were behaving in ways that were going to maximize political damage.

Well, Jesse called them up. Jesse got hold of a copy, gave it to Mary Berry to read—this is what we heard—Mary Berry said to Jess, "It's okay; there is nothing in this report that you can really argue with; you might as well get out front on it." Jesse thereupon called the information officer for the Department of Education and personally requested that they comply with the *Washington Post* request for the report (C. Murray 1980).

But Berry was sufficiently concerned about how the report would be interpreted that she wrote a memorandum to Thomas Minter, second in command in the Department of Education: "I believe a press release should be distributed with this draft report immediately focusing on the positives of the evaluation. In addition, the press officer should sit down with the interested reporters to discuss the report (Berry 1980). Three days later Spencer Rich's article appeared in the Sunday *Washington Post*. Entitled "U.S. Study Faults Jackson's PUSH School Plan," it contained the following:

A new government evaluation of the Rev. Jesse Jackson's PUSH/Excel experiment gives Jackson poor marks on the task of converting this concept into a systematic workable public school program that can help low income students learn better.

. . . The report, the second unfavorable this year, indicates that PUSH/Excel has made some progress. . . .

It is still predominantly an inspirational movement, with the development of specific activities and administrative practices undertaken "in fits and starts . . . or not at all."

Commenting on the report, . . . Jackson said, "PUSH/Excel is a motivation program. It makes no pretense at pedagogy and curriculum develoment."

A Department of Education representative said: "We know that large-scale programs like PUSH/Excel that embrace ambitious missions are very difficult both to implement and to assess in a short period. The effect cannot always be felt for one or two years after implementation" (Rich 1980b).

Unofficially AIR was forced to alter the evaluation by abandoning the incremental evaluation approach that AIR had claimed would help develop the program. According to Saundra Murray,

That decision wasn't ever really made about how much adjusting we should do, and in fact we did make some adjustment. We didn't continue that incremental thing. We couldn't do it. We just couldn't do it. That incremental approach assumes that the program takes your feedback and then makes some decisions and goes on. . . . It became very apparent to me early on that the local sites were not operating in that mode. . . . [The evaluation] was not a systematic analysis of what was working or even putting what was there together in a form that somebody else could come in and help them understand what would work. I think [NIE] would have been willing to go along with the thought of a tailored design for all the sites. We couldn't do the same thing across sites. That was always one of the problems (S. Murray 1982a).

Schwarz's incremental evaluation model foundered on PUSH/Excel's lack of standard, uniform activities at each site. In proposing to apply the model, AIR had assumed that the underlying logic of Excel could be translated into a set of activities sufficiently uniform across sites, that common measuring instruments could be used to describe common activities and measure their outcomes, and that the evaluators could anticipate what these outcomes would be. AIR's descriptions of the programs were accurate but the activities themselves were not uniform; by the time a master blueprint for Excel had been developed, the three remaining sites had developed their own particular models. As these models differed in critical respects from the master blueprint, local sites did not conform to the central plan. As a result, AIR was collecting data to inform local efforts, but local activities were not those being assessed by the evaluation.

By the time this discrepancy had become evident, AIR was already well down the road in its data collection effort, with a set of questionnaires approved by the federal government and a considerable financial, logistical, and intellectual investment sunk in student sampling, permissions from parents, and already completed interviews. Faced with scuttling the evaluation investment or shelving it temporarily, AIR continued collecting data as planned. If the information being collected was too wide of the mark to be useful to local sites, perhaps it would be useful to NIE for avoiding embarrassing questions about the government's $3 million investment in a program sufficiently undeveloped as to be "unevaluable"—unevaluable at least by AIR.

The Third Evaluation Report, April 1981

Thus the data collection continued through the 1980-1981 school year. Interviews were conducted in Chattanooga and Denver, the two sites finally chosen for intensive study, and questionnaires were administered in Chicago as well. AIR considered the spring 1980 data as the "baseline": "Interview data were collected in spring 1980. This was during the second semester of the first demonstration year. However, as previous technical reports indicated, the program has not developed far beyond start-up activities. Thus, we consider these data from spring 1980 as the baseline" (S. Murray et al. 1981, 53).

The third technical report, *The National Evaluation of the PUSH For Excellence Project: Technical Report 3: The Program, the School and the Students* (S. Murray et al. 1981), said that progress was being made in Chattanooga and Denver; that Kansas City and Los Angeles were attempting to reestablish programs; and that Buffalo, New York, had initiated a program using the new *Implementation Guide* to direct activities. Half the report provided an update on local and national efforts during the preceding six months and reviewed the indicators and interview sampling. The second half reported on the "baseline state of affairs" and discussed the implications of the data for achieving the aspirations of PUSH/Excel. AIR evaluators still saw the activities as uncoordinated events involving only minimal effort and commitment and having no explicit involvement strategy (p. 44). They noted from their baseline data that some of the initial student scores were quite high and wondered if the assumption that students had low aspirations was correct. They failed to realize that, as they had collected their data a full semester *after* the programs had started, the students might already have been affected by the rallies, pledges, clubs, and other activities they had experienced.

The press reactions to the third evaluation report were the same as before. This time the news magazines responded. The *Newsweek* of July 10, 1981, ran a full-page article entitled "Jesse Jackson's Troubles." The article cited the evaluation study, and reported that Jackson had lost support on Capitol Hill. One Senate aide was quoted as saying that PUSH/Excel never worked because "Jackson is all talk and no action. [He] is finally getting what he deserves." Another said, "Nobody is weeping for poor Jesse." Jackson himself said that the government grants had given his enemies a boost in destroying his program. He wanted out.

The Final Report, March 1982

The National Evaluation of the PUSH for Excellence Project: Final Report was published in March 1982. A fourth technical report had been scheduled for publication six months after the third report but was waived by NIE because the evaluators had little to add and because NIE and AIR officials were worried about the excessive negative publicity likely to result from yet another pessimistic report. In the *Final Report* AIR assessed the impact of PUSH/Excel upon students in Chattanooga and Denver. Consistent with the original design, indicators of impact were grouped under categories drawn from the basic rationale. In reviewing the level of student involvement in PUSH/Excel, the evaluators concluded that the average student's contact with these activities was so low that the "activities did not add up to an interaction that could be expected to produce measurable effects" (S. Murray et al. 1982, 77).

The evaluators addressed two major questions: Was there evidence of change as a whole? And was there change when the level of participation was controlled? Because clearance of the data collection forms had been delayed within the federal government bureaucracy, the first data collection did not occur until the spring of 1980, even though the PUSH/Excel programs had started in Denver and Chattanooga in fall 1979. Interviews were conducted again in the fall of 1980 and the spring of 1981. However, because of certain unspecified irregularities, according to the evaluators, the data from the fall of 1980 were never used.

From the spring of 1980 to the spring of 1981, there was tremendous attrition in the number of students interviewed. AIR attributed this loss primarily to their inability to obtain permissions from parents. They attempted to interview 550 students in Chattanooga but obtained only 53 student interviews. The interviews contained the primary data for the evaluation. Two of the three schools (Alton Park Junior High School and Riverside High School) were missing entirely from the sample. In Denver, AIR attempted to interview 1,065 students and actually interviewed 223. Altogether in both cities AIR obtained only 276 interviews from 1,615 attempts, or about 17 percent, an extremely poor response rate by the standards of social science research. In addition to the interviews, student questionnaires were collected at Kirkman High School in Chattanooga with a 9 percent return rate.

Not only was the sample of students in the data collection results quite small, it was also highly nonrepresentative. Although the evaluators tried to make a case for the sample being somewhat representative, their case was weak. They compared their final sample in 1981 to the 361 interviews obtained in the predata stage in 1980, not to the 1,615 students they had attempted to obtain originally. This improper comparison would appear to give them a much higher return rate. Furthermore, not only were entire schools missing from the sample, but the racial composition was awry as well.

However, as serious as these distortions were, the most questionable aspect of the evaluation was the data analysis, which was done mostly by Charles Murray, who had left AIR employment by this time but was working on contract. Incredibly, in the assessment of impact the evaluators used the spring 1980 data as predata and the spring 1981 data as postdata. Differences between responses to items in 1980 and 1981 were regarded as evidence of the effect of the PUSH/Excel programs. The problem with this comparison was that the PUSH/Excel programs had already been in operation for most of the academic year *before* the predata were collected. The mass rallies led by Jackson, the pledging of the students, and all the kick-off activities had already occurred. In their own evaluation reports, the evaluators listed dozens of activities that had occurred in Denver and Chattanooga *before* the baseline data were ever collected. Even though many of these activities may have been insignificant, others might well have been expected to improve student attitudes, which were the primary indicators of change in the AIR analysis. The indicators themselves as a method of assessing the program's impact made sense if one accepted the rationale AIR had developed, but the way those indicators were analyzed did not make sense even within the evaluators' own rationale. They had made the most fundamental type of research error.

The possibility that the predata were already contaminated was given credence by the high predata scores on many of the indicators of impact. For example, on a 50-point scale students rated the environment of their schools in the mid-30s on both the predata and postdata interviews. These scores seemed relatively high for this type of school and student, even though the differences between the springs of 1980 and 1981 were statistically insignificant. The lack of change was reported as "no program effect" by the evaluators. Likewise, in predata results, from 60 percent to 80 percent of the parents expressed positive attitudes toward the schools, a seemingly high score. Yet these scores were again reported by evaluators as indicating a lack of effect. (The parent sample was only 10 percent, a worse response than the student sample.)

When 61 percent to 90 percent of the students in each school said that they planned to continue their education after high school, those results were reported to show a lack of program effect because the before and after differences were not statistically significant. For example, at East High School in Denver, 89 percent of the students in the *predata* collection in the spring of 1980 said they planned to continue their education after high school. In the postdata collection in the spring of 1981, 93 percent of the students said they would continue. Because the difference between 89 percent and 93 percent is not great, the evaluators concluded that there was no program effect—although many Excel activities had occurred before the collection of the predata. Even when the student scores reached the upper limits of the scale, as when *all* students at East and Manual high schools in Denver were certain of graduating on both predata and postdata measures, it was interpreted as evidence of no program effect. The impact assessment consisted mostly of such data analyses and interpretations. In my opinion, the data analysis of the impact of PUSH/Excel must stand as extremely poorly done, whatever standards of effective research one might employ.

In most of these schools, drop-outs and absences declined, but the evaluators were reluctant to interpret this information as indicative of program effect because the magnitude of change was slight, in their opinion, and it was difficult to say what events other than PUSH/Excel might have caused the shifts. Altogether the evaluators presented about three dozen indicators and compared the predata to the postdata using tests of statistical significance. Finding few statistically significant differences in the preponderance of cases, they concluded that the program had not had any significant impact. The final results were then summarized in several rows of zeros to give an overwhelming negative impression of the program's results. The evaluators finally concluded, "the analysis reported above did not show a general improvement on the measures that we employed. . . . Such findings would constitute evidence of PUSH/Excel ineffectiveness but for one condition: students in the sample were not exposed to a uniform treatment" (p. 94).

The evaluators contended that student participation in PUSH/Excel activities was very low, averaging only about two activities per student per year. Apparently, however, they did not count activities such as Jackson's rallies or what the students might read in the media. In the evaluators' opinion such participation "did not add up to an intervention that could be expected to produce a measurable effect" (p. 95). But of course this premise was begging the question entirely.

In further statistical analyses the evaluators found that the level of student participation was positively related to the students' certainty of graduating, belief in personal efficacy, efforts to achieve future goals, lowered suspension rates, and higher grade point averages—all positive outcomes. But as these results ran counter to the evaluators' own findings that Excel had no program effects, the evaluators concluded weakly, "when students participate in . . . activities . . . some of them respond in some of the ways that PUSH/Excel hoped" (p. 99). It would indeed be embarrassing to conclude that there was no program but that it nevertheless had had positive effects.

The main difficulties with all the data analyses were that the sample was extremely poor and that the predata were collected a year into the program itself, a procedure so dubious that it threw all the results into question. There were no attempts by the evaluators to draw comparisons with other schools or other students not involved in PUSH/Excel, although such comparisons are common in this type of research. When confronted with these criticisms, evaluator and data analyst Charles Murray responded that there was no PUSH/Excel "program" anyway, so the fact that data were collected at the midpoint of the program didn't matter (C. Murray 1982a, 1982b, 1982c).

Unfortunately, this response showed that he had totally prejudged the question of whether there was program impact. Why bother with data collection at all? The evaluators seemed to have been so completely captured by their earlier conviction that there was no program that they allowed no other possibilities. In their grand summary to the entire evaluation, they concluded: "PUSH/Excel as a program never constituted a 'cause' large enough to plausibly produce an 'effect.'" In my view it would have been more reasonable to conclude from the evidence of their own earlier evaluation reports describing the programs that there were any number of activities that could have produced any of a number of effects.

There is no question that PUSH/Excel had many problems and difficulties in its development. Unfortunately, the final evaluation was so flawed as to leave undocumented whether the program really had any impact on students. Some evidence suggests that it did. And, of course, if there were program effects registered in the evaluators' own data, it would have been rather embarrassing for them in the face of their conclusions that there was no program. In fact, some parts of the AIR evaluation were well done. Events were dutifully recorded, local program histories carefully constructed, and the flavor of the rallies vividly portrayed. For the most part, the evaluators struggled conscientiously with their findings. Ultimately, it was their restricted definition of what a program must be that led to the mismatch between the evaluation and the program itself, the negative conclusions, and the errors of analysis.

8

Reactions to the PUSH/Excel Saga

The political context had changed dramatically by the time the *Final Report* (S. Murray et al. 1982) had been published. The Carter Democrats, who had supported PUSH/Excel vigorously at its inception, had been replaced in the 1980 election by Reagan Republicans. Republican attempts to cut PUSH/Excel's funds and investigate Excel's use of Department of Labor funding ensued. At the local level school districts planned for reduced federal spending on education, and both national and local PUSH/Excel staff saw the handwriting on the wall: federal support would not extend beyond February 1982. The survival of PUSH/Excel would depend on fund-raising.

In the fall of 1981 Jackson informed national staff that hereafter they would be responsible for generating their own funds, but by the following spring only a few staff people remained, and Elma Mardis, the national director, was rarely there. According to Excel's program officer in the Department of Education, Kathlyn Moses, "I think they will keep a skeleton crew at the national office. I really believe that Reverend Jackson is as through with PUSH for Excellence as if it never existed. I think he has gone on to something else now" (Gold and Moses 1982).

When the *Final Report* was published in March 1982, some local programs appeared to be surviving. A local foundation had made a commitment to supplement the Denver school district's funds through 1983, but the program was renamed in one high school and a new wave of staff turnovers occurred at the Denver Excel office. In Chattanooga, a grant from the Lindhurst Foundation was terminated on schedule in the spring of 1982, and Excel program staff members were given pink slips. The district planned to continue PUSH/Excel at a much reduced level, and eliminating the national staff positions placed the program fully under school district auspices. Few were optimistic about the program's prospects after 1983 in either Chattanooga or Denver.

Circumstances had also changed at NIE and AIR. NIE had seen three directors since Patricia Graham's resignation nearly three years earlier, and the agency had finally been eliminated and merged into the Office of Educational Research and Improvement. Some of the former NIE staff remained but morale was low, and Norman Gold eventually moved on to another job. At AIR both Saundra Murray and Charles Murray had resigned and moved on to other positions. From the national to the local level, the education community reeled from a series of actions by the Reagan administration that threatened to curtail programs like PUSH/ Excel altogether.

The final evaluation report received scant attention when it appeared, partly because of its lack of availability: As resources were exhausted at AIR and NIE, few copies of the report were circulated. One copy was sent to the PUSH/Excel national office, one each to Chattanooga and Denver, ten to NIE for internal use, one to the Department of Education, and several copies were retained for AIR's files. The report was never distributed to the 300 people on AIR's master mailing list. Local program personnel, including Excel program staff, received copies at the discretion and expense of their own local districts.

What did receive publicity was the audit of PUSH/Excel finances, which the Reagan administration pursued vigorously. Federal auditors claimed that Excel had received $4,929,847 in federal funds and that $866,713 had been misspent and another $1,302,951 "questionably" spent. The funds at issue included $200,000 in fringe benefits that the auditors considered excessive; $54,000 for personnel who worked on projects not directly related to Excel; and $4,000 for the mailing of Christmas cards.

There were no accusations of any criminal behavior or illegal activities, and Jackson said that PUSH accountants and the federal auditors would work out the differences and that the PUSH/Excel board would repay what was owed. Federal funds are always accompanied by extensive guidelines as to what they can be used for, and it is common for those receiving federal monies to be audited and to have to repay some of the funds. Jackson claimed that such audits were routine (Burton 1987). However, Jackson's operations had been casual about accounting procedures in the past. The news media publicized the federal audit of Excel, particularly after Jackson declared his candidacy for the presidency in 1984. Since then, negotiations have taken place between PUSH/Excel and federal officials, and the latest figure for the amount PUSH/Excel still owes the U.S. Government has been set at $1.1 million (Babcock 1988).

The National Staff: "It Was a Trap"

Reactions to the saga of PUSH/Excel among the principal characters in the drama varied widely. The national PUSH/Excel staff thought that the program had not been given a fair chance to prove its worth. Funding problems, local politics, hostile publicity, and an unfair evaluation were some of the obstacles they cited in interviews. Jackson thought that he was being held accountable for something he had not promised to do. He saw his own job as that of a catalyst: "I came not as an educator, but a preacher. The program was meant to be a partnership. PUSH/Excel was to do the inspiring part, and they (the teachers, students, and parents) would do the rest. . . . If Billy Graham comes to town, people don't accuse him the next week of being inadequate because the local pastor didn't follow through on the newly converted souls." He contended that his proper role was that of a gadfly; it was up to local school personnel to follow through with the opportunities presented to them. He blamed school administrators and teachers for not putting forth the extra time and effort required to make the program work. "There are teachers who come to school as late as they can and leave as early as they can. When they're at school, they're sitting on their can" (S. Smith 1982).

Jackson also thought the program had caused more change than was credited to it. "When you look back at the so-called new school of thought on motivation and self-discipline, all that goes back to PUSH/Excel. The only people attacking the program are its political adversaries." He thought that most of his problems were caused by political opposition, and he was severely disenchanted with the federal government. "We want to phase out the relationship with the government because the government has been more disruptive than supportive. Government grants simply give them the platform to try to destroy the program" (Morganthau and Monroe 1981).

A dramatic change had occurred since the days when Martin Luther King had deliberately planned his marches and demonstrations to provoke the federal government to act, all the time assuming that government intervention could be beneficial to civil rights. And he had been proved correct. Jackson had acquired federal funding through the strong support of the Carter administration, but he had discovered that the silver cloud could have a grey lining. As the *Washington Star* had prophesied five years earlier as federal involvement with PUSH/Excel was being initiated, with even modest federal grants come bureaucratic intruders, stiff guidelines, and meddlesome orthodoxies and ideologies that rub the "sharp edge off the best ideas."

Jackson was not alone in his newly found distrust of the federal government. Thomas N. Todd, a Chicago attorney who later replaced Jackson as president of Operation PUSH, was even more suspicious of the influence of the government: "I vehemently fought against government grants and programs. It is a trap. The requirements are so technical that if you don't dot the i's and cross the t's, you can be cited for a violation. Whenever the federal government wants to move or neutralize they can do it through a regulation" (*Chicago Tribune* 1983).

National PUSH/Excel staff believed that they had been held accountable for not meeting expectations to which they had never really aspired and had not received credit for their accomplishments. In responding to the judgments in the *Final Report*, Mardis, then national director, wrote in a letter to evaluator Saundra Murray:

> No consideration was given to the fact that a program implementation model was developed, put in place and functional. This was simply dismissed along with other efforts to improve the program identified through formative evaluation but dismissed in the summative evaluation. Additionally, no mention was made of program spin-offs which would be indicative of its impact (Mardis 1982).

Mary Frances Berry also wrote to Saundra Murray:

> You seem to believe . . . that one of Jackson's stated objectives was to improve student academic achievement. I recall quite clearly that nowhere and at no time did Jackson ever make such a promise. He instead promised he could motivate students in such a way as to improve the climate in which teachers might improve achievement.
>
> Furthermore, you do discuss HEW's top-down decision to fund Jackson's movement, but you do not note that this top-down decision was obviously not translated into technical assistance and monitoring by NIE staff to aid in the implementation of the movement into a program. You fail to note that Jackson emphasized the necessity for HEW to help in translating his movement into a program before he accepted the offer of federal funds that was pressed upon him. The help never came if your report is accurate (Berry 1982a).

The Federal Bureaucrats:
Marching to the Same Drummer

Federal officials, by this time, still thought the program had potential but had reservations about the methods that had been used to carry it out. Kathlyn Moses, the project officer for PUSH/Excel at the Department of Education, had been in contact with the program on a day-by-day basis from the beginning and through all of its ups and downs. She still thought the program had great potential but that it had failed in its implementation. "I don't know anybody in the United States that does his job as well as Jesse Jackson does his job. Motivating, stirring up, getting the juices flowing, getting the adrenaline glands working. I don't think he has ever thought beyond that point. . . . Somebody had to go in there to do something. You've got federal money, you've got taxpayers' money in there, and I think that is where we stepped in" (Gold and Moses 1982).

Norman Gold, the NIE officer responsible for the evaluation, also thought highly of the program's potential but pointed to flaws in Jackson's personality as the explanation for its failure. In an interview, he said, "PUSH/Excel? I think the ideas are extremely sound. . . . I don't think they thought through the process enough. I don't think [Jackson] learned enough, and I think that Jackson's arrogance was his Achilles heel. I mean it did him in every time. And so he became much too controversial." Gold was convinced that there was indeed a program. "There *was* a program. . . . [It] had a general conceptual framework, and it had some loosely coupled sets of ideas. . . . There was action, [an] enormous amount of action. There were people in place, people in communities and people in schools operating every single day." Although Gold was disappointed that the stakeholder aspect of the evaluation had not been properly carried out, both Gold and Moses thought the evaluation had been helpful to the program. Moses said,

> I think that the evaluation is almost totally responsible for any programmatic aspects that you have for the program. I think that the evaluation was responsible for directing not only national PUSH but the sites and this office to look at program development. I have always thought . . . that it was a tragedy that the evaluation started so soon.
>
> Now I thought that because I am not quite sure that any of us knew what we were evaluating. What we were after. That we understood. And I think that all of us were on different tracks. I think we were all moving, marching to a different drummer. I think the evaluation got us together. So that we were all marching to the same drummer (Gold and Moses 1982).

The Evaluators: PUSH/Excel Never Existed

The AIR evaluators also had strong reactions to the events and their role in them. Charles Murray had been the chief architect of the evaluation design and had conducted the data analysis for the final report. Since his days as an evaluator at AIR, he had gained considerable fame. The Heritage Foundation had hired him to write a paper asserting that tax breaks to the rich stimulated economic growth and that these benefits would trickle down to the poor. Through Heritage's contacts, Murray's paper was quickly picked up by *Time* magazine (April 19, 1982). The Manhattan Institute, a conservative New York think tank, then gave Murray a grant to write a book about the inadequacy of the Great Society's social programs. In the book Murray contended that blacks and poor people were worse off as a result of the federal social programs. The book was a success and Murray was featured in the national media; eventually he debated Jackson on "What Does Government Owe the Poor?" (*Harper's*, April 1986). Murray's personal assessment of Jesse Jackson was not high. And even though he admitted that the evaluation he had designed and helped conduct was seriously flawed, he was resolute in his belief that the program had not existed. In a letter to Gold, he wrote:

> PUSH/Excel *as a program* never had a chance to have impact. It was a non-event from the beginning. . . . We did not "nail" PUSH/Excel.
>
> Let me state very clearly the distinction between two issues. One is whether there are numerous and serious criticisms to be made about the conduct of the evaluation and the impact analysis. The answer is yes, and we should by all means be held accountable for them. The second issue is whether PUSH/Excel—the program—may have achieved effects which the evaluation failed to detect. That the question is even asked reveals how badly we failed to communicate, finally, that PUSH/Excel never really existed.
>
> PUSH/Excel—the movement—did exist and, for a while, was an important element in American education. The evaluation took note of this at some length in every document it produced from proposal through final report. But the federal government did not mandate an evaluation of the movement. It did not fund a movement (C. Murray 1982c).

Saundra Murray had done much of the daily evaluation work. She was the primary author of the reports, had met regularly with local and national program staff to explain the findings, and had served as a liaison between AIR and the federal government. In April 1982, she was still sorting out her feelings: "It was such a disappointment when it was over. So much went for nothing. . . . The first two months were a mixture of guilt and anger. Now I'm trying to make it a positive experience. It was a rough one . . . an experience I can't yet communicate to other people" (S. Murray 1982b). She was a tragic figure caught in the middle. Some of the PUSH staff people called her a traitor to her race; from her own perspective she was trying to fulfill what she thought were the proper professional obligations of the social science evaluator. The evaluation was criticized for the final data analysis over which she had little control (see Farrar and House 1983). She was shattered by the entire experience and thought about pursuing other lines of work;

her aspiration to be the first black woman heading a major evaluation study faded to a pale memory.

Paul Schwarz, president of AIR and architect of the incremental evaluation model, said,

> The PUSH/Excel evaluation was the first one we did since our enlightenment about evaluations, the incremental approach. I think what we've learned from it was that even taking what we thought was a very small bite turned out to be a horrendous first bite. The first intermediate outcomes were far down the pike and never were a key part of the program. They contributed to Schwarz's new first law of evaluation, which is that the inputs never get made. . . . I think an impact evaluation was tremendously premature. An assessment or something early on could have saved the government $700,000 or so (Schwarz 1982).

The Local Stakeholders

The reactions of the local people at the demonstration sites were as varied as the different histories of their local programs. They all perceived failure of some sort but their opinions differed as to whom to blame. Some pointed their fingers at Jesse Jackson. "The night he came to town, it was like a church service," recalled William A. Johnson, president of the Urban League in Rochester, New York. "I just don't think this thing can operate. Jesse Jackson has unparalleled ability to motivate youngsters, but the motivation dissipated when he left town" (S. Smith 1982). James Taylor, associate superintendent of Los Angeles schools, said "Jesse Jackson had a new approach on how to inspire students to study. What was lacking was a new approach on how to make it work. If a program is to excel, it needs more than rhetoric" (S. Smith 1982). In Chattanooga, on the other hand, Malcolm Walker, the in-school coordinator, was proud of what had been accomplished there, as were most Chattanoogans. "Attendance has improved at all six of the schools we have worked with during the two years. Students are more aware of learning . . . We notice more school pride. Students are being more respectful to their teachers" (S. Smith 1982).

In Chattanooga people aggressively confronted the evaluators. Ruth Holmberg, Excel board member and publisher of the *Chattanooga Times*, said, "Why did you keep evaluating this program? You hint in the report that it did not go according to plan, that it was not a systematic development effort that would have been perfect for the kind of evaluation you wanted to do. But you all kept evaluating" (L. Smith 1982). Excel board member Jane Harbaugh commented that the whole program was written up as a futile exercise, like glasses always seen as half empty instead of half full: "You acknowledge that it was something we really couldn't do by talking about the evaluation. Why then would you continue? What you have done is really killed us all" (L. Smith 1982).

Saundra Murray reported a positive attitude at the meeting of Denver stakeholders discussing the final report. "Denver was very good. It was a very large gathering. The tone was one of people with a common interest discussing a set of findings, getting clarification on points, reaching an understanding about what the findings meant educationally, and whose responsibility it was. It was a very, very emotional but attentive group. I frankly enjoyed it" (S. Murray et al. 1982). In Denver the school board agreed to continue PUSH/Excel for another year, but it was institutionalized in a new way. At East High School the name was changed to "E for Excellence," and the main activity was peer tutoring. The irony was that the program was now primarily for white students rather than minorities, and white Episcopal priests rather than black Baptist preachers headed the religious task force. The program was now totally controlled by the Denver school district.

The Media: You Never Can Tell

The mass media largely ignored the final evaluation report. But the damage had been done by the previous reports. PUSH/Excel was already discredited in the public eye, and when Jackson ran for president, the media reported that Jackson was a charismatic leader who could not convert his ideas into reality—an assessment based largely upon PUSH/Excel. Following are typical quotes from the news media both before and after his announcement for the presidency:

> "The initial expectation that through the dynamism and charisma of Reverend Jackson transformation of inner-city schools would occur has not been met," the National Institute of Education said in a report last year (S. Smith 1982).

> The AIR report agreed with a common criticism of Operation PUSH, that Jackson has failed to translate his charisma into a workable educational program (Morganthau and Monroe 1981).

> The study by the American Institutes for Research on behalf of the federal government concluded that the program "turned out to be mainly paper. . . . In reality, PUSH/Excel was still groping for a strategy at the time the demonstration began and it continued to grope through the life of the federal project" (*Chicago Tribune* 1983b).

And from Spencer Rich, the *Washington Post* reporter who had followed the AIR evaluations and prompted anxious meetings at the upper levels of the Washington bureaucracy, the response was a conspicuous silence. Why? In a telephone interview, he said,

> What is left to say? I saw the other reports, and the program was a disaster, a failure. It didn't turn around, did it? I admire a lot of things about Jesse Jackson, and I got tired of beating on him. I think that what the program tried to do was admirable, a good idea, the kind of thing that might work. You never can tell (Rich 1982).

9
The Failure
of PUSH/Excel

By 1982 the national saga of PUSH/Excel was mostly over—an important attempt to improve the education and future of black teenagers brought to an unsatisfactory conclusion. About $4.9 million in federal money and $4.2 million in private funds had been spent on the program. It survived in attenuated form in about twenty schools in Chicago, Charleston, Chattanooga, Atlanta, and Shaker Heights in Ohio. PUSH/ Excel sponsored televised basketball games between black professionals and college all-stars for a few summers, but the national program was only a ghost of its former self, and federal officials were still demanding the repayment of over $1.4 million. As a national effort to institute school reform, the program must be judged a failure. *Why* this failure occurred is a difficult question to answer. There are four possible explanations: They involve Jackson's personality and style of leadership; the intransigence of the public schools toward change; interference and mismanagement by the federal government; and recalcitrant racism.

First, Jackson is an extremely charismatic, volatile, and controversial leader; his worst enemies call him an opportunist. According to this view, there were serious flaws in his character that prevented the program from succeeding, and PUSH/Excel would have succeeded if a more organized person had been leader of the reform effort. Jackson may be superb for inspiring people but not for following through, nor for allowing others to follow through for him. Many whites and some blacks, including most of the government officials in Washington, hold the view that Jackson's personality was the reason for the failure of PUSH/Excel.

The second explanation for the failure is that the school officials were simply not receptive to change, and this intransigence was hardly limited to their attitude toward PUSH/Excel. Reformers are naive, according to this view, if they think that the public schools can be so easily transformed. One variant of this explanation is that schools have routine ways of dealing with "problem" students like black teenagers, and these ways are not about to change because of a little publicity. The schools may appear to cooperate with the reformers, but when all is said and done, black teenagers will be treated as they were before—in ways that control them rather than educate them. And the same resistance to change is true of how the schools approach other students who have been labeled as underclass, mentally retarded, emotionally disturbed, culturally deprived, or different in some other way. The schools are only attuned to routine ways of dealing with the white, middle-class majority of students.

The third explanation for failure involves the interference of the federal government, which initially was unsolicited. Once the federal government started providing funds, a whole new set of demands and obligations was incurred by PUSH/Excel and by the participating schools themselves. Reporting requirements, established bureaucratic procedures, even strong notions about how the program should be operated began to impinge on the program. Under strong pressure, the PUSH/Excel staff adopted terminology and concepts from federal staff members and evaluators and used them in their own documents. These pressures and obligations represented the federal government's technocratic view of the world, not the moral-religious view of PUSH/Excel nor the pragmatic view of the schools.

The fourth possible explanation for the failure of PUSH/Excel is that of overt and covert racism. According to this view, no program that attempts to help blacks is likely to succeed because white institutions are fundamentally racist. Racism is deeply embedded at all levels in the American system, and no amount of rhetoric will expunge it. The teachers, administrators, media, and even the federal government exhibited racial bias throughout this entire endeavor, and in a sense the whole enterprise was a lost cause from the beginning. White majority culture will not tolerate blacks succeeding, no matter what. According to this view, the whole enterprise was a sham, and Jackson was woefully naive in his assumption that such reform was even possible. This view, of course, was held by groups such as the black nationalists. A milder version of this view was that too much racial bias still lingers, albeit unconsciously, for the program to have succeeded, even though the whites involved were well intentioned.

There is an element of truth in each of these explanations, but none fully accounts for the complex chain of events that actually occurred. Rather, I believe that these events reflected certain underlying dynamics of race relations in contemporary America, and the actors played their roles in acting out those dynamics—dynamics that were reenacted in the 1984 presidential campaign. I will explore each potential explanation in turn.

Explanation Number One:
Jackson's Personality and Leadership

Jesse Jackson's controversial personality was the favorite explanation for the failure of PUSH/Excel cited by federal bureaucrats in Washington. In interviews, they said either that he was too arrogant, that he allowed no follow-through, or that his program was constantly disorganized because of his own lack of organizational ability. And there is no doubt that Jackson's personality and leadership were signficant factors in the entire episode. He was peripatetic, unpredictable, volatile, and self-righteous; he was also articulate, inspirational, and charismatic. He did not stay in one place for very long nor with one cause for very long. The enterprise did have enormous problems with organization and follow-through.

The influences on Jackson's personality are remarkably clear as described in the signal biography of him by Barbara Reynolds (1975, 1985). His illegitimacy, his nurturing by his grandmother, his molding by the tightly knit southern black institutions of the church and community, and his early experiences with white racism all help to explain his need for recognition and accomplishment, his drive to lead, his sense of mission, and his outstanding abilities, particularly his rhetorical skills, all of which point to the kind of person who can become a charismatic leader.

These influences explain, in part, his actions and his contradictions, why he is, in his own words, "an imperfect tool" and "a frail vessel" (Reynolds 1975). However, biography and society are mutually shaping forces. I maintain that although personal biography accounts for more than social science allows, ultimately one must examine the social structure in which the individual lives to understand his or her actions fully. I would distinguish between Jackson's personality and his leadership style. Personality derives from personal development, but leadership style is inherited from social institutions. Many of the main events in the PUSH/Excel story resulted from Jackson's charismatic style of leadership, not from idiosyncratic traits.

Jackson's forte is his ability to inspire and persuade large numbers of people and to capture and utilize the media for his purposes, and these abilities were strengths in gaining attention for his projects. But not following through in a programmatic effort was Jackson's main weakness. Hence, Jackson was forever jetting off to another site and another cause, leaving the locals to fill in the details. The very foundations of Jackson's charisma required him to operate in this fashion. This conflict was not merely a personality trait but a necessity of being the foremost leader of the black minority in an overwhelmingly white society. He had to engage the media's attention both to maintain his own prominence and to further his causes. In other words, such leadership style is not simply a matter of personality but a function of his role in American society.

At the same time not just anyone would either aspire to or be capable of charismatic leadership. It takes a particular kind of personality to achieve such preeminence. Jackson's personal background had given him an intense need for recognition, and this desire not only drove him to accomplish a great deal for himself and his people but also drove him sometimes to make mistakes and involve himself in controversial actions. There is no doubt that the single most debilitating event in the short history of PUSH/Excel was Jackson's trip to the Middle East. He was cautioned against it by his own advisors; however, there were reasons for undertaking the trip that went beyond personal whim or the desire for media attention. Jackson's leadership style requires him to take certain types of actions, and sometimes these actions prove detrimental. The complex nature of charismatic leadership will be explored in a later chapter.

The national PUSH/Excel organization never fully organized itself. Mary Frances Berry contended that Jackson said from the beginning that he did not have a developed program. On the other hand, the national office seemed to be in turmoil constantly from beginning to end. It was in conflict with almost every local operation, both the good and the bad, on one issue after another. Promises went undelivered, requests unanswered, and a general dearth of ideas prevailed as to how to proceed. The local sites eventually gave up expecting much from the national office. Furthermore, there was constant turnover in the directorship in the national office. Again, these dysfunctions resulted primarily from Jackson's style of charismatic leadership.

There is no question, in my opinion, that Jackson himself was partly responsible for the failure of PUSH/Excel, although his failure lies more in his particular type of charismatic leadership than in his personality, though of course the two factors interact. In short, the nature of charismatic leadership and the context of its employment were responsible for many of the problems—*as well as for many of the successes.*

Furthermore, attributing all the difficulties to Jackson leaves unexplained numerous events in which he was only marginally involved or not involved at all. For example, why did the schools and the federal government not work around these problems and proceed on their own, merely using Jackson as a catalyst, as Chattanooga officials did? After all, a charismatic leader like Franklin Delano Roosevelt did not personally administer the Tennessee Valley Authority after he established it, nor did Fidel Castro personally eliminate illiteracy in Cuba.

This explanation leaves several unanswered questions. Do schools ordinarily change when reformers other than Jackson are sponsoring the project? Do federal projects without Jackson usually succeed? Do federal evaluations of programs other than PUSH/Excel engender similar problems? Have all remnants of racism disappeared, so that it could be asserted without doubt that it was Jackson personally who elicited negative responses from whites, or was the negative reaction to him because he was black? Even though Jackson and the national office failed to follow through adequately, one must examine the actions of the other institutions for a more complete explanation of the failure of PUSH/Excel.

Explanation Number Two:
The Public Schools

School politics were also critical to the failure of the program. The way Jackson envisioned it, PUSH/Excel would organize the parents, usually through the help of local ministers, and the parents and churches would cooperate with the schools in motivating and disciplining the students. If the schools were not succeeding on their own, then parents could cooperate with the schools to initiate change. But the schools sometimes interpreted parental involvement as confrontation instead of cooperation.

The thought of poor black parents organizing in groups did not sit well with the school bureaucracies. Some key officials were threatened by the idea, and although the ideology of the public schools is that they want public participation, in reality, they do not want autonomous groups of parents or citizens too closely engaged. Like most professionals, educators think that laypeople do not properly understand the workings of their institution, and for the most part school administrators do not want a competing authority system. The dual authority system advocated by PUSH/Excel never caught on, except for in Chattanooga. In one high school the principal simply banned the community liaison from working in the school and used the teacher-advisor for other purposes, such as coaching the cheerleaders. In another high school there were already a dozen parent advisory groups, mostly connected to federal programs. How could the school principal make use of them all? Simply keeping track of them was a chore.

When the PUSH/Excel staff complained about the lack of school cooperation, the program director, a central office administrator, was unwilling or unable to take any action. The principals had considerable autonomy, a common practice in large city school systems. Large city schools routinely develop elaborate devices for shielding themselves against outside influences, out of necessity, one would suppose. Otherwise, they would be at the whim of every organized group. Committed ideologically to public responsiveness, in practice school officials use various tactics to remain in control of their own operations, often appearing to cooperate when they are not. The external pressures on schools are great, especially schools in large diverse cities.

In Los Angeles the new conservative antibusing school board simply lopped off the program from the top, even though PUSH/Excel had nothing to do with busing. In Chicago the district administration appeared to cooperate but offered virtually no assistance. The PUSH/Excel staff tried to do everything on their own—an exhausting and impossible task. In Kansas City the school district never contributed any of its own money to the program, and PUSH/Excel was confined to one school and eventually even ordered out of that school.

Only in Chattanooga were the parents and ministers brought into the program according to the way Jackson had envisioned. Although even there the parents were fully under the direction and control of the school district, participating at the discretion of the school administrators, in Chattanooga all factions of the community did come together to make the program successful. The city establishment was in favor of the program, and the publisher of the local newspaper, a member of one of the ruling families, was a strong advocate. In order to make his program work, Jackson needed the full cooperation of the school authorities but seldom received such full-fledged support. Only in Chattanooga did the system and the power establishment throw its full weight behind the program. Jackson, for all his rhetoric, was unable to force such cooperation if the authorities resisted.

Significantly, too, most of the teachers in the participating Chattanooga schools were black, and Jackson's charisma had an effect upon them, unlike white teachers in other settings who were openly critical. Also the students in Chattanooga were poor blacks and were susceptible to Jackson's influence, and the black ministers were visibly engaged in the program. Quite possibly, much of the enthusiasm for the Chattanooga program was attributable to them rather than to Jackson personally. But Jackson had envisioned the program working in exactly this way, and in Chattanooga, his idea succeeded. The school bureaucracy in Chattanooga was fully and firmly in control. Chattanooga had the most centrally concentrated power structure of all the sites, unlike the more pluralistic power structures in the northern and western cities.

School districts often domesticate attempts to reform them in various ways, particularly when citizen participation is involved, and what happened to PUSH/Excel indicates the limits of Jackson's power and authority over institutions like the schools. Jackson's charismatic appeal was to the masses of blacks, particularly those in the South and those who were regular churchgoers. He could mobilize the black parents to some degree, though not to the extent he had hoped. He also had great appeal to the black students. However, he had little appeal to the white, middle-class professionals who staffed the schools. In fact, they seemed to feel threatened; in some cases the teachers were envious of the working hours and privileges of the teacher-counselors, and school officials were often critical of Jackson's politics. He could focus media attention on the schools for short periods of time, but he could not make the teachers and administrators respond properly.

Consider what it would take to have a successful PUSH/Excel effort. First, there would have to be support from the local school board. Chattanooga, Los Angeles, Denver, and Kansas City had board support for a while, but when the Los Angeles and Denver boards changed, the programs went unsupported. Second, there would have to be strong support at the superintendent's level. This step occurred only in Chattanooga and Los Angeles in the early days but definitely not in Chicago. Third, the school principals would have to be in favor of the program, which was generally true only in Los Angeles and Chattanooga. Fourth, the teachers would have to be in favor, which was mostly the case with the black teachers in Chattanooga. Fifth, there would have to be strong political and financial support from the community; this support disappeared almost everywhere after the Middle East trip, with the exception of Chattanooga.

Change in the schools did not occur from the outside in, nor did it occur from the bottom up or from the top down. The program required strong internal advocates inside the school district to promote it, and the effort only succeeded when the institutional authorities at all levels were willing to cooperate. Unfortunately, everyone had a veto. The school board could stop the program, but so could the superintendent, the principals, and the teachers. Everyone had to cooperate for it to work. This difficult path to changing the public schools is by no means peculiar to PUSH/Excel. All school reforms must pass this gauntlet; few ever succeed. The history of school innovation over the past two decades is mostly a story of failure to change, the same as PUSH/Excel. (See Huberman and Miles 1984; Fullan 1982; and House 1974 for explications of educational innovation efforts.)

Explanation Number Three:
The Federal Bureaucracy

If Jesse Jackson's charismatic power was generally insufficient to effect widespread school reform at the local level, so was the bureaucratic power of the federal government. PUSH/Excel demonstrated once again that one cannot simply push a button in Washington and make things happen in the provinces, or for that matter even in the lower reaches of the federal bureaucracy. The relationship between PUSH/Excel and the federal government was a complicated one. Washington initiated the federal involvement and eventually supplied about half of the PUSH/Excel funds. PUSH/Excel needed the money, but with this beneficence came bureaucratic red tape, a misguided assessment, and eventual condemnation of the program.

The federal involvement was initiated at the top level of HEW, and top officials were confident that the rest of the bureaucracy would go along with such "a great idea." Jackson did not have a well-developed program when Califano and Humphrey pressed their support on him, and lower-level officials were more skeptical. The federal government apparently did not deliver the help with program develoment that it had promised. Legal hang-ups and funding delays also seriously affected the program. Federal support greatly intensified the media coverage, but this publicity proved not to be a blessing in the long run. With government funds came a demand for immediate success. Even when the evaluators wanted to withdraw, they could not do so because of the media attention.

One of the most significant consequences of federal involvement was that an evaluation be conducted. The AIR evaluation was predicated on an underlying industrial metaphor; that is, that a social program is similar to industrial production and should be organized and managed as such. In short, this view required the program to be centrally administered, efficient, and spelled out in minute detail, with every "input" and "output" standardized and predictable. This framework is a common one used in evaluations of social programs, but in my opinion, the AIR evaluators carried this practice to an extreme.

Of course, PUSH/Excel, with its notion of social change as the same kind of mass conversion as in a religious revival, was at the other extreme. The program failed to match the evaluators' model on every count. Such evaluations consider only certain types of reforms with certain specific features as being legitimate. Reforms must have standard sets of activities, be centrally controlled, and conform to the technocratic rationality underlying the evaluations. In other words, such evaluations, in my view, constitute a form of social control; they attempt to control not only the quality of a reform but its content as well. One would assume that social programs subject to such evaluations are eventually forced to conform to this pattern. Otherwise, the programs would be seen as irrational, inefficient, and ineffective, as PUSH/Excel was. In the words of one of the federal officials, the evaluation was invaluable in helping everyone "march to the same drummer."

As the evaluation reports emerged every six months saying the program had failed, that it was mismanaged, that it did not fit the model underlying the evaluation, the national press absorbed the findings and declared PUSH/Excel a failure. National attention was focused on the inadequacies of the program, although the complex underlying basis for these negative judgments could hardly be conveyed in newspaper articles. Not understanding the basis for these judgments, all readers could do was interpret these media stories in terms of familiar stereotypes. Saying that Jackson had taken the federal money and that there was "no program" fit the white stereotype of what black leaders were like. After a few of these reports had been publicized, the program was thoroughly discredited in the public mind and Jackson was seen as ineffective and possibly fraudulent.

Ironically, Jackson tried to change the PUSH/Excel mode of operation because of the evaluation. He hired a national director—Elma Mardis—whom he thought could handle the technical aspects of the evaluation and make the program comply with the evaluators' expectations. Mardis accepted the conceptual framework of the evaluation team and tried to change the program according to their suggestions. However, too much media damage had already been done, and the funding fell through before she could reshape the program to make it conform.

Actually, the program model suggested by the evaluators was far removed from Jackson's symbolic, revivalist notion of change by conversion. One was derived from industrial technology, the other from religion. Jackson and the PUSH/Excel staff never seemed to fully understand the technocratic mentality that lay behind the evaluation. When PUSH/Excel was discredited, he attributed his misfortune to his political enemies who were out to get him. To some extent that assessment was true; he did have political opponents. But I don't think he ever appreciated the fact that he was facing an ideological belief system as deeply seated as his religious one, a belief system equally righteous in its own judgments.

The persistence of this technocratic belief system can be seen in another evaluation undertaken by Charles Murray and AIR at the same time. This evaluation was of the Cities-in-Schools (CIS) program, in which integrated social services were provided for inner-city youths, mostly through the guidance of social workers who provided one-on-one treatment at demonstration sites in Indianapolis, Atlanta, and New

York. The program was a favorite of Rosalynn and Jimmy Carter when they were in the White House.

Although the CIS program was very different from PUSH/Excel, Murray and AIR applied the same framework to evaluate it. Students were expected to demonstrate "investment" and "preinvestment" behaviors, and the ones with the most "assets" were the most successful, according to the evaluation. The CIS program itself was expected to be replicable, fully describable, uniform, and had to conform to written specifications. The evaluation sought to discover generalizable relationships between quantitative indicators that would apply to other programs, but the evaluation study itself provided no way of relating its findings to other research about the problems of these urban youths (Stake 1986).

As in the PUSH/Excel evaluation, the CIS project had problems in the data collection and showed a lack of sufficient data from which to draw conclusions. Yet Charles Murray did draw conclusions, some of which seemed questionable to social science experts, such as a sweeping conclusion that such reform efforts were likely to fail in the future. The final assessment of the evaluation by Robert E. Stake concluded that the evaluation was unfair to the CIS program. The ultimate effect of the evaluation, according to Stake, was to "quiet" or muffle educational reforms and to discourage such efforts in the future (Stake 1986). These problems were all quite similar to those of the PUSH/Excel evaluations.

A final legacy of the federal involvement in PUSH/Excel was that the program was closely audited and the audit exceptions received considerable publicity. By this time the Reagan administration had taken office, and they were intent on a full investigation. Although no illegal expenditures were found, documentation of expenditures was deficient and there were enough questions raised about the finances to cause embarrassment and instigate more negative media coverage. The public could understand the financial problems better than the evaluation results. All in all, the federal involvement did not make for a happy experience.

After Martin Luther King's demonstration in Albany, Georgia, and the failure of the federal government to control the violence directed against the demonstrators there, a woman said to him, "Son, I done found out that even the government is a white man" (Oates 1982, 200). After many years of having the federal government support his efforts, one wonders whether Jackson had similar thoughts when all was said and done.

Explanation Number Four: Racism and Racial Politics

Finally, to what extent is the failure of PUSH/Excel attributable to racism or to racial politics, the fourth possible explanation for the PUSH/

Excel saga? Was Jackson treated exactly the same as if he were not black? The very reason-for-being of PUSH/Excel was to help black teenagers, although the program was open to those of all races. Jackson asked the predominantly white bureaucracy to put forth extra effort to help black teenagers as well as asking blacks to help themselves. It is unlikely that the original federal support would have been given so freely by the liberals in the Carter administration if Jackson were not black or that his project would have been audited by conservatives in the Reagan administration if he were not. So in a sense the program was based on the concept of race from the beginning, although it is impossible to detect reverse racism in the PUSH/Excel materials and activities.

Racial politics were also evident at the local level. In at least three of the five demonstration cities, the program was begun in a context in which considerable conflict had already occurred because of busing for desegregation. In Los Angeles PUSH/Excel got off to an excellent start and was working well by most accounts until the new conservative school board took over, a board elected to prevent busing of students. Even though the PUSH/Excel message was itself Calvinistic and conservative in content, one of the first things the new board did was to withdraw its funds, using the on-going budget crisis as an excuse. So in spite of support among other district officials, PUSH/Excel was eliminated. In Chicago desegregation of schools was also the major issue. And Jesse Jackson and Operation PUSH had already declared their opposition to the voluntary desegregation plan put forth by the school superintendent. In fact, Jackson had been a thorn in the side of the Chicago political establishment for many years, and it was naive on his part to expect their cooperation. The Chicago authorities were more subtle than those in Los Angeles, however. They told the PUSH/Excel staff that they could work in the schools but that the school district was too poor to provide any help, and so the staff struggled to change the schools on their own. In Denver a black school board president initiated PUSH/Excel, but the school board turned conservative while the program was being implemented; the change in the board again was partly because of the issue of busing and desegregation. The result in Denver was that elements of the program were absorbed into the schools and renamed in order to disassociate them entirely from Jackson and his controversial image. PUSH/Excel could claim some credit for leaving something tangible behind, even though it was significantly transformed in both name and clientele.

The greatest blow to PUSH/Excel, however, was Jackson's trip to the Middle East, which effectively wiped out most of his political support and much more besides. In many cities across the country, such as Memphis and New Orleans, plans were abandoned to adopt PUSH/

Excel programs. The Middle East trip both grew out of and exacerbated relations between American blacks and American Jews, and PUSH/ Excel never fully recovered.

Thus racial and ethnic politics had everything to do with PUSH/ Excel. The schools were a battleground for contention amongst racial and ethnic groups. Jackson could galvanize the blacks with his charisma based on the traditions of southern churches but he had little power over the whites, particularly the ethnic whites in the big cities. If anything, his particular brand of emotional oratory threatened rather than persuaded them.

There is a difference, however, between racism and racial politics. Racism has not disappeared from American life by any stretch of the imagination, and occasionally, racist sentiments were heard in the PUSH/ Excel saga. These sentiments were mostly expressed in the context of busing and desegregation rather than about PUSH/Excel itself, which had nothing to do with moving black youths out of predominantly black schools. So at the bottom of some sentiments voiced by opponents of PUSH, there was a smouldering if disguised racism. However, what played a major role in PUSH/Excel was not racism as such but racial and ethnic politics.

A primary part of the ideology of the American public schools is that they are democracy's primary instrument for advancing the cause of impoverished immigrant groups and of homogenizing the disparate groups that populate America into a unified nation—"the melting pot." The truth, in my view, is that American education is entwined inextricably in racial and ethnic politics, in the vying of different social groups for social mobility. Race, ethnic, and class conflict figure prominently in the battle over what the schools should teach, where they should be located, who should go to them, and who should pay for them. And in this general social conflict, PUSH/Excel was no exception. What was unusual was that it made these conflicts explicit, as ordinarily they are disguised within issues like minimum competency testing, educational standards, and school vouchers.

Most Americans would admit that racism still exists. Jackson was not treated *exactly* as a white leader would have been treated, by either conservatives or liberals. That does not necessarily imply racism, however, although sometimes the distinction is a fine one. If one applies the most demanding standard—that Jackson and PUSH/Excel be treated exactly as they would be if they were white—then racism existed. However, the primary forces shaping the saga were racial, ethnic, and class politics, not racism as such. I leave open for the moment the question of the interaction between race, ethnicity, and social class; that issue will be further explored in a later chapter. But clearly, all of these factors were involved in the failure of PUSH/Excel.

In summary, a leader of an underclass racial minority used his charisma to change the education of black teenagers and the schools. The federal government aided this effort, with its attendant technocratic mentality and restricted view of social change, and what resulted was a complex amalgam of racial, ethnic, and bureaucratic politics and the eventual failure of the enterprise. This failure resulted not from the inertia of the major institutions, however, but from their dynamics. These dynamics will be explored in Part Two.

Jesse Jackson and the Power of Charisma

10

Jackson's
Charismatic Leadership

A substantial portion of the difficulties in PUSH/Excel arose from the type of leadership exerted by Jackson, both from the nature of charismatic leadership in general and from Jackson's charisma in particular. It is often difficult to effect widespread social change through charismatic leadership because charisma is specific to one group of people and normally does not extend far beyond that group. The great charismatic leaders—Gandhi, Hitler, Roosevelt—were exceptional not in that they were charismatic leaders but in that their charisma extended to whole nations. Of course, even these men had opponents who were numerous and vehement. How does charismatic leadership work in the case of Jesse Jackson?

Jesse Jackson's most ardent admirers and most impassioned critics did agree on one thing: He was indeed a charismatic leader. In Max Weber's classic analysis of charisma, the term was applied to persons who were endowed with superhuman, possibly supernatural, and at the very least extraordinary powers by which they were set apart from ordinary people and regarded as being exemplary or even divinely inspired. Originally, charisma meant a free favor or gift from God, a grace or a talent that enables charismatic leaders to exert strong sway over their followers.

According to sociologists, charismatic leaders are expansive, dominating, powerful personalities with strong convictions who impose themselves on their environments by their courage, decisiveness, self-confidence, fluency, and energy. They emerge from obscurity into leadership positions in times of crisis and are driven by a strong sense of mission. They generate a collective excitement to which masses of people surrender themselves. People become followers of the cause, carried away by belief and faith in the charismatic leader, and may even turn away from the

117

established social order. As a result charismatic leaders are often disruptive of the regular ways of doing things (Bendix 1962; Shils 1965).

Charismatic leaders often demand obedience from their followers, claiming their authority from higher powers—from insight, inspiration, or divine guidance gained through contact with a transcendent authority of some kind or through identification with a prior charismatic leader. Followers are duty-bound to obey. Charismatic leaders do not necessarily reject worldly goods but do reject regular sources of income; they may live by donations if they are religious leaders, by booty if war leaders, or by political spoils if political leaders. Sometimes they avoid worldly entanglements altogether, and in extreme cases they may reject or curtail family obligations, as in the case of Gandhi (Willner 1984).

They tend to lead loose organizations, the direction of which depends upon their personal insight or favor, and they distribute goods and rewards without being strictly accountable. Their disciples are not assigned highly specific offices or roles to perform, and partly because of this, there is an inherent instability in charismatic movements. Followers often want to make their own positions more secure and to take advantage of the leader's charisma. There is a constant temptation among followers to pull away for the sake of their own autonomy and self-interest, and the leader must constantly demonstrate personal powers to buttress the followers' faith. This validation of leadership is achieved partly through the emotional responses of the followers themselves. Charismatic authority becomes particularly unstable when charismatic leaders die and their organizations must find successors.

Charismatic authority, then, is personal authority, derived not from holding office or social status but from personal traits. At the same time it is based not only on what the leader is like but also on what the followers *perceive* the leader to be like, what the followers need to see in the leader; in short, what the followers themselves are like and what they need that establishes the nature of a particular charismatic relationship. Charismatic leaders often arise in situations in which their people are in crisis; they not only offer a way out of that crisis but often help create and define the crisis as well.

In her study of charismatic political figures, including Gandhi, Hitler, Roosevelt, Castro, and Sukarno, Willner (1984) identified four properties as being the essence of pure charismatic leadership:

1. The leader is perceived by the followers as somehow superhuman.
2. The followers blindly believe the leader's statements.
3. The followers unconditionally comply with the leader's directives.
4. the followers give the leader unqualified emotional commitment.

All of these traits were clearly manifested in the leadership style of Jesse Jackson. He was in some ways a textbook example of the typical charismatic leader. He rose to national prominence as successor to Martin Luther King, another charismatic leader. King had designated Ralph Abernathy as his successor, and Abernathy was acclaimed as such by King's disciples, yet in the crisis following King's death, Jackson won the mantle of black leadership through his own personal talents and the intensive support of the mass media, which projected him as King's successor. Some of King's charisma was passed on to King's widow, Coretta, and to Abernathy, but Jackson gained the leadership.

Enough is known about Jackson's childhood to discern that he fits the description of one type of person who develops into a charismatic figure. He was raised with the peculiar status of an illegitimate son and was publicly known to the community as such. He felt that he was excluded and not respected in the community, and he developed an intense desire to be recognized, to achieve, and to lead. Above all, his childhood associates remembered this drive of his. His half-brother, Noah Robinson, Jr., said, "Most people see Jesse as extremely arrogant, cocky. He's not that way on the inside. He has this compelling need to be recognized. It all stems from his childhood." And his father, Noah Robinson, Sr., said, "As a little man, Jesse told me he was gonna lead. He was talkin' about how he could lead people through the river. I thought it odd for a kid 8 or 9 to be sayin'. But he believed it" (Johnson and Mitchell 1983).

One does not have to be a psychoanalyst to see the motives of Jackson's childhood at work in his adult life. In addition to his tremendous drive to succeed—which might have turned in the wrong direction without the strong guidance of his family, school, and church—Jackson also had outstanding intellectual talent, particularly the skills of oratory geared to generating emotion. He had the opportunity to develop this skill listening to the black Baptist preachers in his youth, and he had a chance to practice it in the civil rights movement. Equally important, he had a chance to learn from Martin Luther King how to attract the attention of the media. King's organization was geared toward staging events for the media that would arouse the conscience of the North and the intervention of the federal government. Eventually, in my opinion, Jackson excelled even King in the use of the media; he sees himself as a producer of dramas for others to enact (Drotning and South 1970).

Many of the typical problems of charismatic leaders are also apparent in Jackson's background. His PUSH organization was loosely managed, and he had a difficult time keeping staff people. They served for a short time, then left, often unhappy with their roles and duties. According to one biographer (Reynolds 1975), Jackson was too insecure to delegate authority or to trust anyone else with much power; perhaps his need for recognition sometimes overcame his better sense of what was effective and what was not. He generated tremendous emotional excitement among his followers for his mission, and sometimes among other people as well. Some of the emotion he incited was negative, but almost everyone, whether they liked him or not, agreed that he was extraordinary.

Sources of Charisma

In order for charismatic leaders to arise, there must be a crisis situation, potential followers in distress, an aspiring leader, and a doctrine promising deliverance (Willner 1984). The leaders might help define the crisis situation, but not just anyone can step forward as a charismatic leader. Charismatic leaders must accomplish four prerequisites: be assimilated to the dominant myths of the culture; perform heroic or extraordinary feats; project remarkable or uncanny personal qualities; and command outstanding rhetorical ability (Willner 1984).

It is critical for charismatic figures to become attached to the primary myths of the culture. This attachment to sacred myths may account for the somewhat mystical quality that surrounds them. In times of crisis, certain myths remain central and sacred to any people with a common culture, and the leader must be assimilated to these. Thus, John F. Kennedy, a glamorous but hardly charismatic figure for most Americans, became a sacred figure *after* his assassination by being assimilated to the Lincoln myth, which is still so powerful in American culture. Fidel Castro was assimilated to the myth of José Martí, the great martyr of Cuban liberation from Spain. Castro's life paralleled Martí's in several ways, either accidentally or through design (Willner 1984).

Jackson succeeded in associating himself with Martin Luther King, the great black martyr. King was not only martyred for his people, but in the minds of many Americans was also associated with the powerful Lincoln myth. The Lincoln myth itself is a manifestation of a more primal myth central to many world cultures, that of a young god or leader who sacrifices himself for his people. Jackson's identification with King was not accidental but was the result of a deliberate campaign— Jackson put his portraits next to King's, affected King's speech cadences, and anointed himself in King's blood, at least symbolically.

A second attribute of charismatic leaders is the performance of outstanding or heroic acts so that they can be seen as heroes or saviors. They must be courageous, or at least perceived as such. The more difficult and risky an action is, and the more it is performed for the sake of the followers, the more the action contributes to the leader's charisma. Certain types of acts, such as rescuing people from dangerous situations, restoring or recovering something valuable that has been lost, and avenging injustices, project the proper image (Willner 1984). It is important that the acts be seen as being undertaken not for one's own benefit but for someone else's.

For example, in Gandhi's great Salt March of 1930, he first notified the British authorities that he was undertaking an act of civil disobedience and then marched hundreds of miles to the sea in defiance of punishment; this action galvanized the Indian people and finally brought the British to serious negotiations. Martin Luther King and his disciples learned to use this same tactic repeatedly in their civil rights demonstrations. In civil disobedience the leader is seen as both personally heroic for facing danger as well as a savior for leading his people out of bondage. Roosevelt was seen as a leader who saved his country from economic disaster; his 100 days of legislation formed a drama of national salvation. That he was from a patrician family only underlined the message that he undertook this action for the benefit of his people and not for himself.

Jackson has followed in the Martin Luther King tradition. The new edition of Reynolds' biography of him, although critical of him, is entitled *Jesse Jackson: America's David.* The reference to David and Goliath makes explicit, as during the 1984 presidential campaign, that the stronger one's opponents, the greater one's heroism and ultimate victory. Jackson has also performed various feats that could be considered heroic, such as obtaining the release of Lt. Robert Goodman from the Syrians, an action that entailed personal risk. In trying to undercut these acts, Jackson's enemies portrayed him as undertaking such actions purely for his own personal benefit. But their concern only showed that these actions were successful in promoting Jackson's image.

A third feature of charismatic leaders is that various unusual personal endowments are projected upon them, as if the followers want or need to believe them to possess traits that are outstanding and extraordinary. Some personal traits, such as extremely high energy levels, personal charm, supreme self-confidence, tremendous determination, and belief in the rightness of the cause, seem to be shared by all successful charismatic leaders. They also project images of working inexhaustibly and of being imperturbable in stressful situations. Jackson shares these traits. The self-confidence of these leaders becomes the "extreme confidence linked to determination or will in the face of seemingly impossible obstacles or the self-confidence linked to the conviction that one is destiny's child chosen to accomplish what others perceive as an impossible mission. Those possessing and expressing this sort of assurance often seem to many to be close to madness or genius" (Willner 1984, 146). Sometimes this self-confidence is punctuated by periods of self-doubt, but any lapse in confidence is shared only with intimates, not with the public. In America such extreme self-confidence must be leavened with self-deprecating humor or else the person is perceived as arrogant—a label often applied to Jackson.

Other attributed personal traits have nothing to do with leadership directly but enhance the leader's supernatural image. For example, Sukarno was projected as a man of voracious sexual appetites, which had nothing to do with unifying Indonesia in any direct way. Gandhi, on the other hand, was known for his vow of sexual abstinence, which he took at age thirty-seven and maintained until his death at age seventy-eight. Within the Indonesian tradition Sukarno's sexual image enhanced his reputation, and within the Indian tradition Gandhi's image of chastity enhanced his. The interpretation of particular traits depends upon the culture (Willner 1984). Jackson has the image, whether justified or not, of leading a life among celebrities and "high rollers," which his biographers claim enhances his reputation within the black community.

A fourth ability shared by charismatic leaders is that they are eloquent and spellbinding orators. They have a rhetorical talent that goes beyond the message they are conveying. They use figurative language extensively in their speeches—metaphors, similes, analogies, images, and allusions— the full range of rhetorical devices employed by public speakers for centuries. No contemporary American needs to be persuaded of Jesse Jackson's rhetorical ability; he is probably the best orator in the land. In fact, many of the best American orators have evolved from the southern black Baptist traditions of evangelical preaching.

Jackson uses numerous allusions to the Bible, as did Roosevelt in his famed speeches. Roosevelt employed references like Mammon, money-changers, false prophets, the plague of locusts, and even terms like crusade, pledge, covenant, and promised land, as he applied biblical imagery to the problems of the nation (Willner 1984). In contrast, his opponents often used imagery taken from the world of business. Both Jackson and Roosevelt made extensive use of alliteration, assonance, rhyme, rhythms, repetition, irony, and humor. Compare Roosevelt's "Hardheadedness will not excuse hardheartedness," from his Second Inaugural Address in 1937 to Jackson's "No one can save us for us but us" from the PUSH/Excel crusade. This kind of rhetoric displays strong moral overtones, which places the leader in positions of moral superiority to their opponents.

Although rhetorical ability of this sort is the single factor most closely allied with charisma, there are many great orators who are not charismatic, and reportedly Gandhi was not a spellbinder. Great rhetorical ability is not sufficient by itself. One must also possess the other three factors, or at least most of them—assimilation to the dominant myth, the performance of heroic feats, and unusual personal qualities. Of course, these are merely categories of academic analysis. To generate charisma all these factors must be woven into the mosaic of a message or doctrine in order for the appropriate charismatic effect to be produced. The integration of these factors into a mission is what generates charisma. I turn now to the overall mosaic within which the followers perceive charismatic leaders, for it is their perception that is the critical factor.

A Moral Order

All people have a need to see themselves in the midst of an ordered cosmos; it is their place in that order that gives meaning to their lives. They need rationally intelligible maps of the world that provide coherence, continuity, and justice: Their world view must include moral order. Religions often provide such a world order for people. Charisma can be seen as a response to great ordering power, a power that arouses emotions of awe and reverence and sometimes generates a charismatic response (Shils 1965).

The extraordinary quality of charismatic leaders, according to this view, is derived from their perceived contact with this ordering power, or vital force. Contact with this force takes place through a symbolic event, which can occur in a number of ways. Leaders regularly claim legitimacy because of contact with another charismatic person, because of tradition, because of their insight into fundamental truths or ethical imperatives, or because of the will of their followers, as demonstrated by acclamation (Shils 1965). Jackson's charismatic authority is based on all these sources. The most explicit was his claim to be the disciple and successor to Martin Luther King.

Much less appreciated by whites is Jackson's authority as a minister. This qualification is important among blacks. The Baptist church traditionally had been the strongest institution in the black community, and the black minister holds a position of great influence and status. When Jackson is mentioned in the mass media, the ministerial title is often dropped, but blacks are keenly aware that Reverend Jackson is a man of God, not just another social commentator or politician. Martin Luther King, of course, was also a minister. The black Baptist church has been Jackson's main basis of popular support throughout his career. It was through the black ministers in Chicago that he organized political action against the Daley machine and the boycotts against various corporations. Jackson took great pains not to offend black ministers, even to the point of holding the weekly PUSH meetings on Saturdays rather than Sundays, when they might compete with services in other churches. He supported and publicized other ministers through his media outlets, and they in turn gave strong support to him.

This church connection helped Jackson in several ways. Through the church he had a permanent power base. White observers were puzzled by his ability to survive the withering media assault on him after his trip to the Middle East. If his influence had been based entirely on the media, he would not have survived this episode as the preeminent black leader. The church and its ministers provided a basis of power that remained intact, and he could ride out these public relations mistakes with their support. The church gave Jackson high visibility and money, and he had strong appeal to black Americans where the church was strongest—in the South and other areas where there were rural blacks. Given his contact with King and his support through the church, Jackson was—and still is—the most visible unifying force in the black community, crossing class and regional lines.

Contact with King and his position as minister are two bases of Jackson's charismatic authority; a third is the need for moral order that he fulfills for people. His message is both moral and political, and his pithy slogans place his followers squarely on the side of moral rectitude. Jackson's presence and eloquence, his rhythmic little sayings, have great appeal to large numbers of people, black and white. In a world of complex problems and hopelessness for poor blacks, Jackson provides simple solutions, just as Ronald Reagan has provided simple solutions for large segments of the white population.

After King's death, blacks were looking for leaders, and they wanted to believe that Jackson could solve their problems, that he had the understanding and will to see them through. He exuded confidence and determination, even in his physical appearance. At a time when Americans had lost confidence in many of their institutions, they looked for strong leaders. In slogans like "I am somebody" or "No one will save us for us but us," Jackson encapsulated a sense of mission, direction, and supreme confidence. At a time of confusion, Jackson was a generator of certainty and moral order par excellence. This trait was a primary source of his charisma, especially insofar as it extended to whites. The important role that Jackson had as moral commentator and his reliance upon the mass media as the stage for his preaching meant that he had to constantly appear in the media to comment on national issues. His followers needed repeated performances from him to ascertain their place in the world, and as a charismatic leader he needed to repeatedly display his powers in order to maintain his following. As a result, he was forced constantly to jump from one issue to another; whatever subject was popular in the media, there went Jackson's attention.

Crowd Emotion and the Use of Rhetoric

A fourth source of Jackson's charisma was the will of the people, which was demonstrated visibly not through elections or polls but through public meetings. Jackson was regularly seen in the media exciting large crowds of people, whether it was at PUSH's Saturday morning services, in the Superdome at PUSH/Excel rallies, or in political speeches registering voters. An important element of his charismatic appeal was that he aroused people emotionally and was seen by others as having the power to do so. Crowd response validated his leadership.

Jackson learned his rhetoric and moral lessons in the black Baptist church. The church was a sanctuary for a troubled and persecuted people, and through it there was hope. Martin Luther King, Jr., more reserved and middle-class than Jackson, had finally succumbed to the emotional power of the church, as described by King's biographer.

At first his sermons tended to be sober and intellectual, like a classroom lecture. But he came to understand the emotional role of the Negro church, to realize how much black folk needed this precious sanctuary to vent their frustrations and let themselves go. And so he let himself go. The first "AMEN!" from his congregation would set him to "whooping" with some old-fashioned fireworks, in which he made his intellectual points with dazzling oratory. For what was good preaching if not "a mixture of emotion and intellect?" As a preacher in his own right, free from entanglements with his father, King learned to appreciate the southern Negro church as never before. Here in their church—the only place that was truly their own—black people could feel free of the white man, free of Jim Crow, free of everything. Here they could be spiritually reborn and emotionally uplifted, exhorting their preacher as he in turn exhorted them, both engaging in a call-and-response dialogue that went back to their African ancestry. And young King, observing this at Dexter, seeing now what he had been blinded to in his youth, became a master at call-and-response exhortation. "And I tell you [tell it, doctor] that any religion that professes to be concerned with the souls of men [well awright] and is not concerned with the slums that damn them [amen, brother] and the social conditions that cripple them [oh yes] is as dry as dust religion [well]. Religion deals with both heaven and earth [yes], time and eternity [uh-huh], seeking not only to integrate man with God [clapping, clapping], but man with man" (Oates 1982, 56–57).

In crowds people can feel equal (Canetti 1960). They can abandon their man-made distinctions of rank, status, and wealth imposed upon them by their social order and throw off their differences. This moment in which weighty social discriminations are discarded and all feel equal is the moment a crowd is created. No one is better than anyone else, and all the distances that separate people are overcome. Thus, the emotionalism of fundamentalist churches appeals particularly to those low in the social hierarchy. All charismatic leaders have particular appeal to the lower social classes. And as we have seen, no one was better at exciting a crowd than Jesse Jackson, "The Country Preacher."

Institutionalization of Crowd Emotion

Of course, the moment of crowd ecstasy is transitory. As soon as the crowd breaks up, social distinctions reassert themselves and distances between people reappear. Only in permanent conversions can people give up their old associations and elevate themselves to a new life. And only a limited number of people are able to achieve this permanent transformation because continuance requires rules and some form of institutionalization. The personal transcendence offered by the crowd is temporary. But with an institutional structure it can be reassembled and its emotions rekindled (Canetti 1960).

Social institutions like churches represent efforts to domesticate the crowd and direct its activities. The notion of a crowd out of control, like a lynch mob, elicits a particularly chilling response from most people, unless they are part of the crowd itself. Institutions like churches funnel crowd emotions into established channels, and through repetition, ceremony, and ritualized performance, they provide a sense of unity, equality, and fervor while at the same time keeping crowd emotions within well-regulated boundaries.

The Catholic church is particularly adept at regulating strong emotions; its rites and rituals dilute emotion and its measured, slow processionals arouse veneration rather than stronger passions. Its ceremonies hamper communication among worshippers so they cannot incite each other, and even the Communion is directed at introspection rather than at the group. The feelings aroused are between the individual and the church; stronger emotions and the commonality of feeling engendered by other crowd activities are restrained. By being enclosed in churches, Catholic worshippers attain a sense of unity but are also highly constrained (Canetti 1960).

Not all churches are like this, however. Emotion is a primary appeal of fundamentalist churches. The most outwardly emotional church of this type, perhaps, is the Pentecostal church. The Baptist church is also one of these, particularly the black Baptist church. There are indeed ceremonies, but in contrast to Catholicism, many fundamentalist ceremonies are designed to incite crowd emotion rather than restrain it. Communication between worshippers is encouraged, even to the point of congregants shouting out in ecstasy, calling to the preacher, and in the Pentecostal churches, speaking in "tongues." Perhaps the culminating point in the church service is when the converts step forth to declare themselves for Christ—mass conversion.

Another device that generates crowd emotion is rhythm. Any type of rhythmic activity—songs, chants, clapping, stomping, dancing—intensifies the emotional experience, particularly if the crowd itself participates. According to a leading black folklorist, black church songs are always based upon "dance-possible" rhythms (Hurston 1983). Shouting, seen as a favor from the spirit, is an "emotional explosion" evoked by rhythm, which can be sung, spoken, hummed, clapped, or foot-tapped. "Shouting is a community thing. It thrives in concert. It is the first shout that is difficult for the preacher to arouse. After that one they are likely to sweep like fire over the church" (Hurston 1983, 91). And the more familiar the expression, the more likely it is to evoke a response. Jackson always began and ended his rallies with the chant "I Am Somebody."

Another way to incite crowd emotion, as Jackson found, was to use an arena, like a sports arena. The arena provides a double crowd. Not only can the crowd experience excitement, but people in the crowd can see that others also are excited (Canetti 1960). Spectators in a closed ring, shut off from the rest of the world, become excited by one another's behavior, as at a sporting event. The excitement feeds on itself; all is enclosed and thus intensified. The physical layout of the structure can actually contribute to the excitement. Arenas and stadiums are scenes of great emotional rallies, such as those that initiate PUSH/Excel programs. One middle-class man who attended the PUSH/Excel rally in Denver said, "You think you're above all that, but I found myself up on my feet shouting along with everyone else."

Deliverance from Oppression

Within an emotional crowd there is absolute equality, which is the reason why people want to be part of the crowd. Demands for justice and equality derive energy from the crowd experience (Canetti 1960). Despots ban or control behavior for it can incite revolutions, but charismatic leaders make excellent use of crowd assembly. Having a common goal reinforces feelings of equality and extinguishes individual goals for the moment. The crowd needs direction; it must have a goal to maintain its existence. The leader gives the crowd this sense of direction; in this kind of crowd leadership Jesse Jackson was unexcelled.

"The art of a speaker consists in compressing all his aims into slogans. By hammering them home he then engenders a crowd and helps to keep it in existence. He creates the crowd and keeps it alive by a comperhensive command from above. Once he has achieved this it scarcely matters what he demands" (Canetti 1960, 331). Slogans are indispensable to certain types of crowds; they provide direction. The direction in which Jackson led was toward deliverance: At the end of the Rainbow Coalition was not a pot of gold but collective deliverance from the indignities and privations that poor blacks had been suffering at the bottom of the American social hierarchy. Jackson's slogans were concise messages of deliverance—"I am somebody"; "No one can save us for us but us"; "Our time is now!"

The type of crowd Jackson engendered is called "reversal" crowd; reversal crowds are dominated by a passion for either revival or revolution (Canetti 1960). In a moral reversal such as a religious revival, deliverance from the problems of the world is expected to occur only in heaven, and the sufferers must pass through death and be "revived" to be delivered. Those who are saved must first admit that they are fallen and then be "new-born." The role of preachers is to terrify the listeners with threats of God's wrath, then to offer them the way to salvation. They are delivered from their own worst selves. Religious conversion results in obedience to God's commands.

By contrast, reversal crowds with revolutionary intent come into existence for the liberation of a large number of people who have been beaten down and cannot reverse the situation by themselves. The goal is liberation from the demands of a dominant social group. The crowd unites against its oppressors, and the perceived oppressors become afraid because of the pent-up hostility directed at them. This hostility is most effectively expressed when it can be focused upon one person, toward a king or a president, for example (Canetti 1960). A revolutionary reversal can only occur in a stratified society in which a group of people are subjected to commands from those above them. In order to rid themselves of this long-term domination, this "sting of command," they band together to throw off their yoke in a collective effort. The crowd believes it can do together what its members cannot do singly. Once started, this process of reversal is contagious.

Jackson's PUSH/Excel program was based upon the revivalist notion. Students were to master self-discipline, with the help of their parents, teachers, and preachers, and through this self-discipline, they would be delivered from their indulgent selves and be reborn as upwardly mobile members of society. The mass rallies were directed to this end, and Jackson was the absolute master of the slogan of reversal—"From the slave ship to championship"; "From the outhouse to the White House!"

Because PUSH/Excel's educational activities were revivalist rather than revolutionary, members of the establishment, including even political conservatives, were willing to support PUSH/Excel at first. Perhaps they saw it as an alternative to some more revolutionary activity that might be directed at them. However, many of Jackson's political activities were ambivalent in nature; these activities aimed at uniting blacks against their oppressors, and it was the thin line between these two possibilities that made many whites vacillate about PUSH/Excel. When Jackson traveled to the Middle East and embraced Yasser Arafat, he crossed the line for many whites, who withdrew their support and tried to disassociate themselves from Jackson. Although Jackson repeatedly stressed his non-violence, mass rallies steeped with emotion engendered fear in many whites, who felt that *they* were the targets of a potentially powerful reversal group.

Our Time Has Come

Every significant social group has myths that set it apart from other groups. In fact, these myths provide a primary means by which a group identifies itself as separate and distinct. Myths are sacred histories that recount the origins of the group in some distant past. For example, one of the myths that binds Jews together is the story of the Exodus from Egypt. The entire people wandered in the desert for forty years, suffering many privations in their search for the promised land. This image of a people united in migration pursuing a common goal where they would be delivered still unites Jews. It was natural that a man as well-versed in the Bible as Martin Luther King would use the myth of the promised land as a symbol for the deliverance of American blacks. This image suggested a long, ongoing travail with much suffering still ahead. The goal was distant rather than immediate, and the day of deliverance was delayed until sometime in the indefinite future. This myth was reassuring not only for blacks—explaining their suffering and prophesying its end—but was also comforting to the whites who did not feel so threatened by a distant future. In contrast, Jackson did not often invoke the symbol of the promised land. Instead, he was seen by whites as impatient as he demanded, "We want it all" or "Our time has come!" Jackson preached a more immediate deliverance, one which threatened whites.

Jackson invoked another powerful myth. Religions of lament, like Christianity, have at their core the legend of a man or god who dies unjustly before his time (Canetti 1960). He is mourned and lamented by his relatives and disciples; his death may be pictured in concrete detail, with wounds and blood graphically portrayed. The lament adopts the theme that the dead man has died for the sake of the people who mourn him; he was their savior. Not only is his loss irreplaceable, it is also unjust. Such lamentation can engulf a large crowd.

This myth is enshrined for Americans in the life, mission, and death of one of their most sacred figures—Abraham Lincoln. His assassination has been told and retold in such detail that it has become a unifying force that gives emotional meaning to their existence as a people. His trip to the theater, the assassin sneaking up behind him undetected and shooting him in the head, the oozing wound, the turmoil, confusion, and grief, and the slow funeral train back to Springfield draped in black is told to every schoolchild. The quintessential American poet Walt Whitman wrote, "When lilacs last in the dooryard bloom'd, And the great star early droop'd in the western sky in the night, I mourn'd and yet shall mourn with ever-returning spring." Few legends are as powerful for Americans as the story of this martyr to national unity.

The continuing emotional power of this myth was revived in the death of John F. Kennedy. The young man, the leader of his nation, was struck down unjustly, shot in the head, his brains and blood splattered over the dress of his wife; again, his wounds were graphically portrayed. His wife and young children mourned him publicly; his young son saluted his father's casket. The family was joined by millions of mourning people, including leaders of other countries. He was the martyred president, and the lamentation for his death was intense. People from other countries shared this grief not only because Kennedy was the leader of the Western world but because other peoples share this myth.

In the words of a British historian:

> There is one contemporary American myth, however, that does have an almost universal magic. The force of it is conveyed in two pictures that still have undiminished poignancy.
>
> In the first frame, a youthful President, hatless in the cold air, rededicates a new generation to whom the torch of idealism has been handed.
>
> In the second, the same head is blown to pieces by a bullet (Hodgson 1976, 4).

Similarly, Martin Luther King, Jr., the leader of his people, the Nobel Peace Prize winner, was struck down by an assassin's bullet. He was shot in the head, part of his jaw was blown off, his wounds were graphically portrayed, and the blood was smeared symbolically on the shirt of Jesse Jackson. King was martyred, declared the savior of his people, and publicly mourned by family, disciples, and millions of people around the world; his death was seen as an unjust tragedy. His life took on sacred meaning, and those associated with him shared this sacredness to some degree.

This myth of lamentation for the young man or god struck down unjustly before his time can be a rallying device to mobilize a group of people to action. In fundamentalist Christian churches the myth of Jesus, the son of God, struck down unjustly in order to expiate our sins, is the rallying point for persuading people to step forward and be "saved." For His sake one must convert, not only to save oneself and be reborn but to justify His death. He died for us.

President Lyndon Johnson used the myth of the martyred Kennedy to pass the Great Society legislation through Congress. Passage had been blocked under Kennedy himself, but after Kennedy's assassination it was passed within days. Similarly, Jesse Jackson used the myth of the martyred Martin Luther King to mobilize black Americans. The myth placed an obligation upon them to justify King's unjust death. They no longer wanted to suffer a long delay, to wait anew for the promised land. Rather, the marytr had paid the price, had endured the suffering. Blacks had been redeemed and reborn; the long-suffering travail had been transformed by the myth into "Our time has come!"

11

The Limits
of Charisma

The advantages of charismatic leadership are far-reaching. The charismatic leader can galvanize and mobilize large numbers of people, and charisma is particularly effective in increasing the political activism of those who are inactive and apathetic. All the charismatic leaders discussed—Gandhi, Hitler, Sukarno, Castro, excepting only Roosevelt—came from societies that had rigid class and status structures (Willner 1984). All were extremely popular with the underclasses, who had been inactive and politically dominated, and even Roosevelt exercised his charisma at a time when a large number of his countrymen saw themselves as downcast and forlorn.

One of the effects of charismatic leadership is to lessen the sense of social inequality among followers. Part of the increased activism stems from the followers' enhanced view of themselves. They begin to see themselves as politically more efficacious and as worth more than the respect accorded them by society. Charisma releases pent-up energy, at least for a limited period of time, and the Roosevelt administration as well as the regimes of Castro and Sukarno were marked by tremendous vitality and social action that went far beyond mere mobilization. In these cases such activity prompted a renewed sense of national identity, in which the downtrodden reinvested their confidence in the state (Willner 1984).

Leaders who have charisma have advantages in exercising their authority. They can order followers to do things simply because the leader says so (Willner 1984). Hitler could establish the SA and, when he thought it harmful to his cause, order it disbanded and expect his order to be obeyed on the basis of his personal authority, which it was. This control over followers gives leaders greater flexibility in charting policy directions, as they can change direction with a minimum of cost and explanation; they can advocate one policy one day and another the next. Such control provides additional leverage in political bargaining, as one can establish positions purely for bargaining purposes without having to cement them with one's followers.

Jackson's mode of operation was certainly marked by great mobilizing power, supercharged energy, intensified political activism, sweeping reversals in policy, and successful bargaining for jobs and business. His leadership brought renewed hope and vitality to the cause of the black minority by focusing national attention on problems and issues important to blacks. These were substantial benefits.

Despite these advantages, charismatic leadership also has its limits. The key question for charismatic leaders is how far their charisma extends, for these limits severely affect what they are able to do. No one is charismatic for all people, and significant social change requires the cooperation of many participants. The status of the followers is also important (Willner 1984). A leader who has influence among the powerful has enhanced means for accomplishing given ends. Furthermore, the rules of the particular social system limit what can be done. The reach of Jackson's charisma in PUSH/Excel was quite limited, and he did not develop other means for pursuing his objectives. His constituency was limited to people—mostly black students and black teachers—who did not have much power within the educational system. Jackson was not charismatic even for the power structure in Chattanooga; to them, he was simply another black preacher-leader. The elements that created Jackson's charisma within the black community did not have similar purchase across the general population. Even though his assimilation to the Martin Luther King myth was recognized by all Americans, the attachment of the King myth to the Lincoln legend was not accepted by all whites. Jackson's status as a minister was also nonconsequential for most whites. The crowd emotion and the rhetoric of the black church were fascinating to whites but also strange and unfamiliar, reinforcing white perceptions that he was "their" leader.

Feats of bravery, such as his rescue of Goodman from the Syrians, were dismissed as "grandstanding" or as being purely in Jackson's own interest because Goodman was black. "He would never have done that if Goodman were white" was a common response among those I've talked to. Also, Jackson's image as being something of a "swinger" never enhanced his reputation among whites. In fact, it probably reinforced their stereotype of black morality. All this criticism was only based on his image, of course, but one's image is critical to charismatic leadership. The very factors that enhanced Jackson's charisma among blacks did not have equal influence with whites.

There was one area in which Jackson did have purchase on the white imagination—his advocacy of a moral order that cared for the poor and the dispossessed. However, instead of pursuing the general theme of the downtrodden, Jackson understandably turned to the particular injustices perpetrated against blacks. This appeal to black audiences mitigated against any sizable constituency among the whites. If Jackson were to build a white following, he would have to pursue broader themes and appeal to whites who saw themselves in similar situations. He did not do so during the PUSH/Excel period and did so only sporadically during his 1984 presidential campaign. All these factors limited his appeal and his consequent influence. His greater degree of success in the 1988 presidential campaign was due, in part, to the fact that he did begin to pursue broader themes.

Finally, there are some absolute disadvantages of charismatic leadership, that not only limit influence but which can have pernicious effects as well. These disadvantages include a certain amount of endemic disorganization, the possibility of virulent backlash, and a lack of accountability. Almost all charismatic leaders disdain formal organization. In the administration of their national governments, Roosevelt, Hitler, and Sukarno all set up agencies with overlapping authorities, fuzzy jurisdictions, and poor coordination. They assigned different agencies competing tasks and often divided control of an enterprise among several different people. They proliferated new agencies and governing bodies and preferred to establish new initiatives as opportunities arose. Roosevelt's creation of New Deal agencies is an example of this tendency, and throughout his regime Hitler encouraged competing agencies with overlapping jurisdictions to pursue the same task.

This style of administration seems deliberate rather than an oversight. By setting up rivalries and confusion among their subordinates, charismatic leaders seek to ensure control and force others to be dependent upon them. Only they can resolve the ensuing conflicts. One might make a case for the efficacy of certain types of deliberate disorganization, especially when dealing with large bureaucracies, but on balance disorganization is clearly a disadvantage. Of course, this lack of organization, or perhaps the choice of disorganization, was a significant factor in the problems of PUSH/Excel. Put simply, the organization was seldom able to follow though on its plans and promises.

A related problem was illustrated by Thomas Todd, one of Jackson's strongest supporters, who said, "We were raising issues and not following through on them. We'd raise the issue of black colleges . . . then move on to South Africa. I made a mistake, I was wrong in my evaluation of PUSH's role. [Jackson] cannot and could not solve the problems that he raised. But he can focus attention on an issue. He can bring it to the national consciousness" (Johnson and Mitchell 1983). At one time Todd resigned from the PUSH board because of Jackson's gadfly behavior but finally came to terms with Jackson's role as moral commentator—a role essential to his charisma. The charismatic style of leadership at Jackson's disposal required him to gain the attention of the media but also limited him mostly to persuading others to act to ameliorate social ills rather than organizing and directing well-wrought attacks upon social problems himself.

There are two other serious problems with charismatic leadership—the strong backlash it sometimes engenders and the potential lack of accountability. People who incite very strong positive emotions in some people also incite extremely negative emotions in others, which means that an intense backlash against charismatic leaders is not unusual. Another problem is that it is very difficult to call to account, in any conventional sense, leaders who believe their lives are divinely inspired and that they are destiny's children. In part it is this absolute certainty of the leader that transfixes followers. Both of these problems were manifested in PUSH/Excel but were far more pronounced in the presidential campaigns, for the dynamics of Jackson's charismatic leadership were not limited to his educational program but were in fact an integral part of the general framework of black/white relations in America.

Charisma as Power

Charisma can be regarded as a form of power, power being, in Bertrand Russell's words, the capacity to produce an effect. Political "power is the capacity of some persons to produce intended and foreseen effects on others" (Wrong 1980). With the exception of Chattanooga, Jackson's PUSH/Excel program did not produce the effects he had intended and that others expected, and part of this shortfall was attributable to the type of power at his disposal.

In Wrong's analysis of power relationships, he describes five types of authority: coercive, induced, legitimate, competent, and personal. Coercive authority rests on the threat of force of some kind. Induced authority consists of rewards that one might offer people for their compliance with what one wants them to do. Legitimate authority rests on obligations based upon collective norms, such as law or tradition. Competent authority is based upon belief in an authority's special competence, as when one listens to a physician's advice because of presumed expertise. Finally, personal authority is based upon the authority's personal qualities, the person's personal significance to the others. And the most "extensive" of all personal authority is charismatic authority, the sway of one person over a large number of people on the basis of personal characteristics.

These types of power relationships differ in their extensiveness, comprehensiveness, and intensity. Extensiveness refers to the number of people affected. Comprehensiveness indicates the range of activities that are affected. For example, an advertisement may be very extensive in that it communicates with many people but not very comprehensive because it affects only a tiny area of people's lives, such as the toothpaste they buy. Intensity refers to what limits there are to what the authority can demand of the "power subject." How far can the bidding of A be pushed without B failing to comply?

Coercive, induced, and legitimate authority are relatively high in extensiveness, comprehensiveness, and intensity. Depending upon one's resources, one can coerce or induce a large number of people to do many things. By contrast, competent authority, such as that of a doctor or teacher, is exercised over many people but is restricted to narrow ranges of activity and is narrowly constrained in the activities that the authority can demand of the power subject. Finally, personal authority can be exercised across a wide range of activities and with considerable intensity, but it is ordinarily restricted to only a few people. There is one exceptional form of personal authority, however, and that is charismatic authority. Charisma exceeds all other forms of noncoercive power in its comprehensiveness—the range of activities—and intensity—how far one can go. Charisma can affect a large number of people as well. It is "personal authority in its most extensive form" (Wrong 1980, 63).

Of course, these definitions of power and authority are highly idealized, and an actual situation ordinarily encompasses more than one power type simultaneously. In fact, it is to the advantage of a power holder that he or she broaden the types of power used, because different people respond differently to the various types. In dealing with the school bureaucracies Jackson was forced to rely upon his charismatic authority and persuasion, the latter being a form of influence in which one presents arguments and the other person evaluates them. Persuasion entails an egalitarian relationship, whereas the five types of authority entail command-obedience relationships. Persuasion is based upon the *content* of the communication, whereas authority is based upon the *source* (Wrong 1980).

Jackson had little coercive power (or else chose not to use it in PUSH/ Excel, as boycotts and demonstrations, which he had used earlier, are a form of coercive power), little induced authority, and no legitimate authority, such as law or tradition, except that which he might derive from the involvement of the federal government or the endorsement of the school system itself. Being a minister gave him legitimate authority in the black community but not in the white establishment of the school districts. He did not use PUSH to picket or boycott the schools or engage in other coercive behaviors, as he had in the civil rights movement and in dealing with corporations, when his economic campaigns had been based upon boycotts organized through the churches. These boycotts entailed coercion and inducement with a considerable amount of moralizing thrown in. And the strategy had been highly effective.

With PUSH/Excel, Jackson could offer the participating schools only a small amount of money derived from private donations and the federal government. Instead, he relied upon his charisma, and although the blacks involved were greatly affected, the white bureaucracies were essentially unmoved by his charisma, based as it was on the myths and rituals of Martin Luther King and the black church. The whites had their own myths and rituals, and Jackson was not playing their tune. For the most part their response was lukewarm, sometimes even hostile.

On their side the school bureaucrats had legitimate and competent authority. They were the official, legal office holders charged with operating the schools. Furthermore, they believed themselves to be possessed of superior competence and expertise in educating children—thus, they had competent authority. When they looked at the PUSH/Excel advisors and community liaisons they saw people without educational expertise, and they were not about to cooperate with unqualified laypeople. They held to their belief in their own competency and legitimacy, they had the power to withhold cooperation, and they did.

Only in Chattanooga, where the power establishment and the school system put their full legitimate and coercive weight behind the program, did it succeed. This authority was manifested in the Advisory Committee that was organized to run the program. Furthermore, the teachers in these schools were mostly black and southern-born, and they were susceptible to Jackson's charisma. They were willing to take PUSH/Excel seriously and try to develop it. In addition, the students in these schools were black and poor, the ones most influenced by Baptist ministers like Jackson.

Ultimately, then, the frequent lament that PUSH/Excel "had no program" was in part a protest that the PUSH/Excel people had insufficient competent and legitimate authority to change the schools. This protest came most often from the school authorities themselves and from the official arbiters of legitimacy, the federal evaluators. In the eyes of many of these people the program was not properly "authorized." Of course, the school authorities and the evaluators had quite different ways of judging the program's legitimacy.

In short, the form of power that Jackson employed to effect his great social reform for black teenagers was insufficient to do what he intended.

It was effective with many black adults and students, less effective with black teachers, and ineffective with white teachers and bureaucrats. His charisma was truly effective only with people who had no power of their own to transform the system. The financial inducements were also weak, although they did play a role in inducing some districts to participate. Only where full legitimate and coercive authority was invoked in behalf of the program did it succeed. Perhaps Jackson always expected the authority structure to support the program fully; in any case he chose not to use coercive power as he had in the past.

What would have been required in order for the program to result in success? In a study of school politics in Chicago, Peterson (1976) identified the combination of political resources necessary for community control advocates to win concessions from the school system. PUSH/ Excel was not a community control endeavor, but the two situations were similar enough that the example is instructive. As Peterson tells the story, in 1966 an education group at the University of Chicago proposed to the U.S. Office of Education that an experimental school be started in the all-black Woodlawn section of Chicago next to the university. That neighborhood already had a strong community action organization, the Woodlawn Organization founded by Saul Alinsky. The Woodlawn Organization heard about the proposal and objected that the community had not been consulted. The Office of Education returned the proposal and suggested that the university experts consult with the public schools and the community.

Eventually a tripartite governing board was established consisting of all three groups—the schools, the community, and the university—and a new funding proposal was submitted to the Office of Education. The Office of Education had successfully used its inducement powers to gain cooperation among these three major entities. However, the Chicago schools still would not have cooperated without the university, in spite of the enticement of federal money and the power of the Woodlawn Organization. From the beginning the school district engaged only reluctantly in the planning of the project. Although the superintendent, James Redmond, expressed verbal support, he took no initiative to assist the project and said no local money could be used. The project administrator chosen by the superintendent also expressed strong reservations about community involvement. When the plan was submitted to the Board of Education for approval, the superintendent would not endorse it, arguing that the board would not accept the plan. At the board meeting the school attorney expressed doubts that it was legal for the school board to delegate its governing powers to a tripartite governing body, and several school board members also expressed reservations.

Superintendent Redmond had let the proposal progress as far as it had because of his friendship and respect for Roald Campbell, the dean of the School of Education at the university. The university had played a mediating role between the other two groups. Now, when the school attorney demanded that the school board be the sole authority, the University of Chicago threw its legal staff into the struggle. After numerous meetings it was agreed that the community board *could* govern legally. The project was in operation for several years, and reportedly many changes were introduced into the Woodlawn schools as a result. Eventually the Nixon administration took office and the project funds were cut in 1973. Without federal money and endorsement, the project folded—a familiar story. Throughout the life of the project, school board members continued to oppose the sharing of authority and questioned the legitimacy of involving the Woodlawn Organization.

In his analysis Peterson concluded that three things were necessary for the project to succeed, even for a limited period of time: the availability of federal funds and federal pressure to cooperate; a strong community organization like the Woodlawn Organization that insisted on being included; and the involvement of the University of Chicago, which provided access to the school system and legitimacy among educators, not to mention legal competence. All three were crucial to success. Without the legitimacy provided by the university—both competent and legitimate authority—the school district would never have cooperated. All five forms of authority were employed, including the personal, although charisma did not seem to be a major factor.

Jackson, the PUSH/Excel staff, and the federal bureaucrats expected the local schools to cooperate much more than they did, but their authority was based only upon Jackson's charisma and federal inducements. It came as a surprise when the schools and ethnic political groups responded negatively with their own forms of power. Jackson's charisma reached the limits of its ability to effect change in the face of competitive countervailing forces.

PUSH/Excel relied too heavily upon the expected cooperation of the existing institutions. The PUSH/Excel organization lacked legitimacy derived from being perceived as competent educators. Jackson consistently underestimated the feelings of professional competence among the educators and the technical expertise the evaluators possessed, all at PUSH/Excel's expense. Jackson also underestimated the strength of other ideologies which legitimated the actions of both school officials and evaluators. The PUSH/Excel enterprise was seen as nonprofessional, amateurish, and nonlegitimate.

One way around this debilitating perception and lack of cooperation would have been to join forces with organizations already possessing competent authority, such as universities or state education agencies. Jackson's charisma was not of much utility because the authority derived from technical and bureaucratic expertise excludes charisma as nonrational. To put it more starkly, some would say that bureaucrats cannot be converted because they have "no soul." In fact, the bureaucrats, evaluators, and educators each had their own belief systems and ideologies—beliefs far removed from those of PUSH/Excel.

PUSH/Excel as Civil Rights Movement

Jesse Jackson's attempt to change the schools in such a way that they would be more conducive, stimulating, and beneficial to black youths grew out of the civil rights movement and used similar tactics. The PUSH/Excel people were experienced with the goals and strategies of movements, and they understood the world in those terms.The movement of the 1960s had translated movement activities into substantial and tangible gains—such as voting rights, affirmative action, and jobs—but PUSH/Excel, using the same methods, could not effect such changes.

Minority movements work something like this (Omi and Winant 1986). First, the intellectual leaders—the preachers, teachers, journalists, professors, artists, and entertainers—raise the level of consciousness of the mass of people by focusing on injustices, repression, and fundamental deprivations that minorities suffer compared to the majority population. They challenge the existing racial ideology that legitimates the social order and the low status of the minority group. By creating a different explanation, a counter-ideology as it were, the leaders mobilize the mass of people behind their efforts to create pressure on the government institutions. It is in this mobilization and definition of the problem that charisma plays an important role.

If the pressures are intense enough, the government responds by instituting reforms. These reforms might be absorbed into the governmental procedures in moderated form or perhaps restricted to areas that are symbolic and not central to the government's operation. The reforms instituted might or might not make any difference as far as the welfare of the people is concerned. Some elements of the social movement might be absorbed into the government to administer or regulate the new reforms and other elements become radicalized because the reforms do not go far enough. A new era of quiet stability and equilibrium is reached until the next reform effort.

Social movements mobilize their supporters by creating a new collective identity for the group that is significantly different from the majority, received view. This new collectivity, or collectivity with a new identity generates new demands. In the civil rights movement of the 1960s, this intellectual leadership was provided by black preachers and students preaching from pulpits and leading marches in the streets. In PUSH/ Excel this leadership was provided by Jackson, with other preachers, teachers, entertainers, and athletes following his lead. This movement, they hoped, would result in a transformation in the way black teenagers saw themselves, in a new collective identity.

At first the black teenagers did seem to respond, but the crusade shattered against racial politics, against the unresponsiveness of the schools, against a negative and corrosive federal evaluation, and upon the inability of the PUSH/Excel staff to develop a more systematic program. The schools did not respond in such a way as to make continuance of the program possible, and apparently the teenagers could not maintain enthusiasm and dedication or redefine themselves without the cooperation of the key institutions. Jackson had approached the problem as a matter of mobilizing energy and effort, but had underestimated the power of the existing institutions to resist pressure and disallow redefinition.

Charisma can do certain things. It can mobilize but it cannot organize. It can fill the Superdome with enthusiastic people but it cannot transform the structure of the school system and its day-by-day operations. PUSH/ Excel began as an extrainstitutional movement, much praised by everyone, and when all was said and done remained extrainstitutional. Without the cooperation of the major societal institutions, the redefinition of self and new collective identity that Jackson had called for never materialized.

In short, charisma by itself was simply insufficient to do the job. In her examination of the effects of charismatic leadership, Willner wrote,

> Political charisma in and of itself has rarely, if ever, been sufficient to accomplish a complete reordering of a system or a revolution. . . . If one were to rank charismatic leaders of this century solely in terms of the magnitudes of changes they accomplished, Hitler and Castro would rank high. Much of their success, however, resulted from charisma plus force, and some of the charisma may have been sustained only because possibilities of dissipating it did not exist (Willner 1984, 192–193).

12

The Politics of Race and Social Class

The puzzle of where to place the frustrating story of Jesse Jackson's PUSH for Excellence within the perennial enigma of race and racism in American society remains. Any satisfactory explanation of the PUSH/Excel saga must not only be consistent with the specific events described but must also address some difficult questions, such as the following. All of them, directly or indirectly, are ultimately related to the concept of race.

- Why is Jackson the way he is?
- Why are there questions about his accountability?
- Why does Jackson employ a charismatic approach to leadership?
- Why didn't he use a different leadership style altogether?
- Why couldn't Jackson make deals with the schools as he did with corporations?
- Why did the southern, hierarchical Chattanooga power structure cooperate with PUSH/Excel more than those in the northern and western cities?
- Why did several school districts start the program then stop it?
- Why did some people object to voter registration in particular?
- Why did the schools resist the intrusion of parents?
- Why are the schools so difficult to change in matters like those with which PUSH/Excel was concerned?
- Why did the evaluation employ such a technocratic approach?
- Why did Jackson's Middle East trip cause such a debacle?
- Why are the schools the focus of so much ethnic and racial politics?
- Why do these ethnic and racial groups become political?
- Why do we have racism at all and why does it continue?

Three Conceptions of Race

There are three main ways of interpreting race in contemporary America—the ethnicity-based conception, the nation-based conception, and the class-based conception (Omi and Winant 1986). A fourth conception, that of race as biologically based, is older than these three and occasionally rears its head, as in the eugenics movement or in explanations of intelligence-testing differences associated with educational psychologists like Arthur Jensen. For the most part, however, contemporary Americans subscribe to one of the first three conceptions. The following descriptions of these views are based on Omi and Winant's 1986 book, *Racial Formation in the United States*. Which of these three conceptions is most consistent with the saga of PUSH/Excel?

Ethnicity-based Conception

The concept of race as ethnicity sees blacks, Asians, and Native Americans as ethnic groups, the same as Italians, Poles, Irish, Germans, and so on, who will soon be assimilated into mainstream American life. This view is based upon the history of European immigration to this country. Immigrants who entered as separate and distinct groups at different times were eventually assimilated into the mainstream of society and most of their ethnic characteristics disappeared. It is presumed that the same will eventually happen to blacks and other racial minorities. The ethnicity conception challenged and replaced the older biological conception of race, which held that people of other races were not only different from whites but also inferior. Even though the biological conception sometimes makes a reappearance, the ethnicity view ascended to dominance in 1944 with the publication of Gunnar Myrdal's *An American Dilemma* and has remained the dominant interpretation of race in America since that time (Omi and Winant 1986).

In the 1920s Robert E. Park from the University of Chicago's Department of Sociology formulated racial assimilation as a law of historical development and postulated the stages of contact, conflict, accommodation, and assimilation. This formulation included the idea that the most important aspects of racism were individual attitudes and prejudices, and also that racial assimilation was inevitable (Hughes et al. 1950). The civil rights movement developed from this new perspective. Once blacks obtained safeguards and privileges such as voting rights and education, it was believed that they would be assimilated into the mainstream.

In the 1960s, however, the ethnicity view was challenged with arguments that the European experience was different in important ways from what the other racial groups had encountered. Blacks, Asians, and Native Americans had remained unassimilated for very long periods of time, and sometimes did not seem to be making the progress toward full assimilation at all. The response to this challenge was a new version of the ethnicity view put forth by scholars such as Nathan Glazer and Daniel Patrick Moynihan (1963), who argued that some ethnic groups had not been assimilated into the mainstream because their own social and cultural norms were different, mostly deficient; they thereby portrayed cultural norms or values as powerful independent causes of social and economic fortune. For example, some of these ethnic groups did not value education as highly as the more successful groups did.

According to this view, group differences in social achievement and wealth were the ultimate result of group norms. Individuals from these disadvantaged groups were prevented from achieving what they might otherwise achieve because of their own values. Later the neoconservatives argued that group differences would disappear when and only when these ethnic groups adopted the norms of the larger society. Group norms and values, they said, were what impeded progress, not racism or other societal impediments. Group norms were seen as internal to the group itself and not the fault or responsibility of the larger society.

The neoconservatives were opposed to satisfying minority demands for group rights. No collective equality for groups should be pursued, they said, only equality for individuals. Government and society should be colorblind, concerned only with individual rights, not group rights. Privilege and social position should be awarded on the basis of individual merit, not group membership. Policies applying to opportunties for groups, such as affirmative action, were strongly opposed by neocon-servatives who, in short, opposed any type of racial collectivity (Omi and Winant 1986).

Perhaps the apogee of the neoconservative view was expressed by Charles Murray, the PUSH/Excel evaluator, who argued in his influential book *Losing Ground: American Social Policy, 1950-1980* that the liberal social programs and policies of the federal government had in fact destroyed the proper work norms of the black underclass, thereby making them lazy and undisciplined. The social programs, he said, had caused blacks to become increasingly poor and disadvantaged.

Nation-based Conception

A second major conception of race in America is the nation-based perspective, represented in the writings and activities of people such as W.E.B. DuBois, Marcus Garvey, and Malcolm X. This conception sees blacks in America, and other races as well for that matter, as victims of European colonialism. Institutions in the United States, according to this view, are in reality a continuation of the subjugation of colonial peoples by white Europeans. This perspective in particular caused some fracturing in the civil rights movement, which was based mostly upon the ethnicity view.

Some civil rights leaders, such as Stokely Carmichael (renamed Kwame Ture), popularized the term "black power," converted to a black nationalist view, and embraced Pan-Africanism. Carmichael ultimately returned to the United States to raise money for guns in an effort to free South Africa and unite the African continent under black leadership (Sandrock 1987). The examples of W.E.B. DuBois and Marcus Garvey indicate that this separatist conception is of long historical standing; but the Black Muslims, who espouse a strong form of black power and separate identity, best typify this black nationalist approach. The movement today is led by such leaders as Louis Farrakhan, whose association with Jesse Jackson caused great embarrassment.

Fundamentally, the black nationalists see racial dynamics as derived from colonialism. Those who hold this view see one nation or people systematically exploited by another. Social classes or other subdivisions within those groupings are secondary or not important. And unlike those who espouse the ethnicity view, the nationalists do not see any desirability of merging as one more ethnic group into the larger American culture. Such assimilation is a recipe for permanent subjugation and exploitation, in their view. The white liberals of the civil rights movement found this nationalist position difficult to accept, as it implied total separation of the races.

Class-based Conception

The third conception of race, one that has challenged the dominant ethnicity viewpoint but never replaced it, is that racial discrimination is based on socioeconomic class structures. Differences between races are a function of the economic structures and processes in society, according to this view. Different economic structures in each socioeconomic class produce different outcomes, so that economic class and position are more fundamental to one's life chances than race. Within the class-based conception, there are different explanations as to how this class differentiation operates, ranging from the ideas of neoclassical economics to the class conflict explanations of the Marxists. Although the class-based theorists all see inequality among socioeconomic classes as fundamental, they differ considerably about the dynamics and direction of this class differentiation. And, of course, social and economic class position are external factors, in contrast to cultural norms, which are usually seen as internal to the group under consideration.

One recent version of the class-based conception has been advanced by sociologist William Julius Wilson (1978), who has pointed out that the black community itself is dividing into an advantaged black bourgeoisie living outside the ghetto and a black underclass deprived in every way still living within the ghetto. Until 1965 blacks had been treated as a separate caste, but about this time they were admitted into the society-wide stratification system, which is to say that they became stratified by economic class within their race just as the whites. In this view the black underclass is becoming worse off as a large gap is opening between the black middle class and the black underclass. In other words, middle-class blacks, although still subject to racial discrimination from time to time, have much better life prospects than underclass blacks. Social class has become relatively more important than race as a determiner of life chances and in fact, I believe, underlies race relations.

The PUSH/Excel View

PUSH/Excel was a direct outgrowth of the civil rights movement and was fundamentally based on the ethnicity conception of race. If black youths could only reform themselves through effort, hard work, and education, they would be successful and be accepted in the larger American society. Others did not always see PUSH/Excel as fitting this conception of race and, in fact, saw it as a black nationalist movement, and some opponents of PUSH/Excel criticized it for being too radical. From its own perspective, however, the PUSH/Excel effort was not a radical attempt to reform the system at all, even though it was an unusual one. Fundamentally, Jackson accepted the idea that if black youths worked hard, earned good grades, and succeeded in school, they would be rewarded with success in the larger society. The responsibility lay with them, not with the system, and thus, the solution would not be found in a radical restructuring of the system.

Instead, an improved education was the way to attain success in the larger society. This belief fit the dominant societal view of race relations: Blacks were like every other ethnic group preceding them; they differed only in the norms of hard work, diligence, and individual responsibility. If they only adopted the norms of the larger society, they could get ahead. Racism, social class, and other barriers were not insurmountable. This belief also fit in with mainstream American thought, which viewed changes in attitudes as the most important prerequisite for assimilation, as the ethnicity view prescribed.

On the other hand, the actual tools for reform that Jackson had in hand were American but definitely not mainstream. He had an organization, staff, and experience born out of the 1960s civil rights movement.

The tactics for reform were extrainstitutional—confrontation, rallies, sit-ins, marches, media attention, and the rhetoric of deliverance. His leadership style was strictly charismatic—emotion, not routine; rhetoric, not paperwork; persuasion, not edicts. That is how black leadership had evolved after several centuries of slavery and one century of freedom.

PUSH/Excel acted according to the ethnicity paradigm but the American institutions did not. The crusade shattered against racial-ethnic politics, the unresponsiveness of the schools, a negative federal evaluation, and the inability of PUSH/Excel to develop a more systematic program. The schools did not respond in such a way as to make continuance of the program possible. Jackson had approached the problem as a matter of personal reformation aided by the schools, the families, and the community but had underestimated the power of the existing institutions to resist reform.

The neoconservative attempt to preserve the ethnicity view of race placed the blame entirely on the inadequacies of Jackson and the PUSH/Excel staff concluding that PUSH/Excel was simply not competent to develop such a program. In fact, the evaluation designed by neoconservative Charles Murray declared that there was no program, but this explanation, although it fits the ideological structure of the evaluation itself, does not explain the responses of the schools and the racial/ethnic politics surrounding PUSH/Excel that affected the fate of the program so dramatically yet had nothing to do with the content of the program itself. Nor, of course, does this explanation account for the flaws in the evaluation. That is to say, this explanation does not account for some of the events that most heavily influenced the PUSH/Excel story.

A second explanation is suggested by the black nationalist conception of race; namely, that the entire enterprise was a ruse meant to hold blacks in colonial bondage. Such an explanation would account for the eventual failure of the enterprise and for some of the actions of the schools and also for some of the racial/ethnic politics. For example, it would account for the desegregation politics, the withdrawal of support after the Arafat affair ("These people must abide by *our* foreign policy not their own"), and the lack of enthusiasm from white teachers and administrators.

However, a black nationalist perspective would not account for why and how the program began in the first place, why it was successful in southern cities like Chattanooga, why some blacks criticized it as well as Jackson himself, nor for the many efforts exerted in its behalf by both blacks and whites. Furthermore, to regard the entire enterprise as a ruse, one would have to presume a degree of planning and scheming on the part of governing white elites. In short, both the ethnicity and nationalist conceptions of race leave many of the PUSH/Excel occurrences unexplained.

Social Class

The Ultimate Grouping

The conception of race as ultimately class-based, in my opinion, provides a much better framework for understanding the entire PUSH/ Excel story. First one must recognize the schools as arenas of contest for the various social groups in America. The schools are a major avenue for economic and social advancement within society and are seen in that light by average citizens on an everyday basis. Hence, the schools are the focus of intense social conflict among the diverse social groups that make up contemporary America.

This view of the public school system is not entirely consistent with either the ethnicity or nationalist conceptions of race. The ethnicity view does indeed view schools as major avenues of advancement but does not anticipate the conflict among social groups as they contend for access and control of the schools in order to advance their own interests *at the expense of the interests of other groups.* As Jackson envisioned it, the schools would simply help poor black children who helped themselves because the schools were there to help anyone who needed help. But, in fact, the schools did not do so. Likewise, the black nationalist conception of race would anticipate that the white-controlled schools would only maintain the exploitation of blacks. The schools did not follow this path either. In fact, the schools were willing to help but *only* on their own terms.

The ultimate reason, I believe, for this phenomenon is not that the schools were particularly inert or exploitative but that the schools were trying to accommodate other social groups. That is, if they changed too much to accommodate PUSH/Excel and the black students, they would have trouble with other social groups whom they were serving. And by other groups, I mean other social and economic classes. Other groups and classes were already actively striving to increase educational advantages for their own children. Any major deviation from the ongoing procedures would result in conflicts with these other social groups, who also thought the schools necessary for their own advancement. It was not that the other groups blatantly wished harm to the black children or their future prospects, it was just that these other groups were concerned for the prospects of their own children. The ultimate reason, I think, that schools never seem to change very rapidly or dramatically is that such changes always run afoul of some particular social group.

That is to say, the current arrangements favor social groups who already have influence with the schools, namely the middle classes.

Socioeconomic classes were the ultimate grouping because the future economic and social life prospects of the students—that is jobs and economic livelihood—were at issue here. Often these concerns are expressed or registered by specific racial or ethnic groups, but when all is said and done all groups want to ensure their opportunities for better jobs and social position. The material interests of the groups themselves are always at stake in regard to educational issues. The life prospects of students are determined more by their social class than by either their ethnic group or their race. The reason the schools are so important as arenas of contest is that, increasingly, jobs are allocated through educational credentials. Educational advantage converts directly into economic advantage.

Class and PUSH/Excel

Once one accepts this class-based framework, the events of the PUSH/Excel saga make more sense. The reason some school districts initiated the program then reneged was that the school board membership changed so that different class interests were represented; this change usually stemmed from a backlash to desegregation efforts. Resistance to busing can be regarded not so much a matter of white parents not wanting their children to go to school with black children as those parents wanting their own children to obtain an education that would enable them to reap educational advantages and hence economic ones. Put another way, perhaps these white parents would object far less to black children being bused several hours to the white schools than to their own children being bused to the black schools; the white parents saw the latter case as putting their own children at a disadvantage.

As long as the school districts did not have to reduce the quality of education of the other children, parents would find a program like PUSH/Excel acceptable. That is why the federal money was so important, even though the grants were small in comparison to the size of these large city school budgets. To use funds from the regular school district budget would take resources away from the other students, whereas additional, specially designated money from outside could be spent for this purpose. Furthermore, according to this explanation, the voter registration ceremony PUSH/Excel advocated was particularly resented because it seemed to grant additional political influence to a competitive group.

Schools resist parental intrusion into their internal affairs because they are so intensively besieged by parents to provide educational favors for their children in one way or another. Middle-class parents regularly visit schools and teachers, and thus often gain favored treatment for their children. Working-class and underclass parents are too intimidated by the schools to acquire equal access. Large city school systems in particular have developed mechanisms to buffer themselves against outside influences, although of course such insulating devices are not totally effective. To be responsive to external community demands often means to be responsive to the wishes of the upper social classes who are more demanding.

The more pluralistic the city, the more diverse the groups in contention and the more difficult it is for the schools to satisfy everyone. It was in the largest and most pluralistic cities that PUSH/Excel was begun, in response to the demands of a particular interest group, and quickly discontinued, also in response to pressures from competing interest groups. To put it another way, the interests of middle-class groups eventually prevailed over those of a lower-class group, the advocacy of the federal government notwithstanding. The federal government itself was acting on behalf of this disadvantaged group, as it often does, although the federal evaluation did not serve that advocacy in the long run. Evaluation itself presumes to serve as an impartial balance for the adjudication of these diverse group interests.

The interests of the middle class do not *always* win out over the interests of the lower classes, and the PUSH/Excel case is no exception. The PUSH/Excel program would never have gotten started if middle-class interests always win out. However, over the long run and on average, middle-class interests prevail most of the time, in spite of legislation, court orders, and federal advocacy. The schools resist change not because of their own inertia or indolence but because it is in the interest of various social groups to keep them the way they are; this rule operates not so much to suppress blacks or the underclass as to retain the advantage for the dominant class.

The Politicization of Ethnicity

Of course, the most cataclysmic event of the PUSH/Excel story was not the formal routine difficulty of changing the schools but Jackson's trip to the Middle East. How could this incident possibly reflect class interests and be explained by a class-based conception of race and racism? To put it simply, class interests often appear in the guise of ethnic interests. In order to compete successfully in the battleground of American interest-group politics, groups find it greatly to their advantage to organize themselves collectively. In fact, it is almost impossible for large groups to advance their interests any other way. And in order to organize themselves, they often draw upon their own ethnic identities. This phenomenon has been called the "politicization of ethnicity." "This means simply to use ethnic patterns and prejudices as the primary basis for interest-group and political formations, and to build upon these to integrate a given ethnic community into the wider politics of the city and nation" (Kilson 1971, 336).

For example, groups like the Irish, drawing upon their common heritage, took over the political machines in the large cities of the northeast and even came to support the war in Northern Ireland against the British government in an extension of their collective identity. The Sicilians, faced with being excluded by Irish politicians, utilized the Mafia to further their interests. All disadvantaged groups in the United States are eventually forced to organize themselves in such a fashion because other competitive groups are already well organized in order to help themselves. Groups who do not do so, like the poor Appalachian whites both in the Appalachian Mountains and in the large cities, remain impoverished and politically ineffective. Needless to say, the dominant classes do not like to see other competing groups succeed in organizing themselves.

Jackson went to the Middle East to demonstrate symbolically the cohesiveness and independence of American blacks, just as the other ten black leaders had tried to demonstrate when they visited the Middle East ahead of him. They wanted to show that the most prominent black public official, Andrew Young, could not be summarily dismissed without consequence just because he opposed Israeli/Jewish policies. The explosive nature of the clash between American blacks and American Jews over this issue was particularly intense because both groups saw the event as absolutely critical to their own group identity and interests. American Jews had not only organized themselves around their own unique religion, tragic history, and ethnic background but saw the nation of Israel as the virtual embodiment of this collective identity. This collective identity had not only allowed them to advance themselves economically and socially to become one of the most advantaged ethnic groups in American society, but had enabled them to *survive*; this survival as a people was symbolized by Israel and thus, Israel was not something they were likely to compromise.

In contrast, the blacks saw the Andrew Young affair as a return to one-sided plantation boss politics. They had advanced a leader, which was symbolic of their rising status and fortunes in society, and as soon as they expressed an independent opinion they were slapped down. For them, Young's firing confirmed their worse fears that their newly won political power was a sham, and they reacted strongly. The intense clash of minority groups, which extended into the 1984 and 1988 presidential campaigns, will undoubtedly arise again. Underlying this clash is the fact that blacks and Jews are coming into increasing economic competition over jobs and commerce, and as a sizable black middle class emerges, many of these contested jobs are professional and managerial. Their collective identities will be enlisted in the ensuing conflicts over social and economic position. The current disagreements over affirmative action policies are the current focus of this emerging contest.

Jewish-Americans and Irish-Americans are currently influential enough to affect American foreign policy both in Israel and Northern Ireland. At the other extreme, one does not hear much about the Appalachian-Americans' concern over Margaret Thatcher's policies regarding Scotland and northern England because the Appalachians are not at all organized. Blacks are only now becoming somewhat influential on policy regarding South Africa. In short, the reason Jackson went to the Middle East was to galvanize the collective interests of American blacks, and the reason the American Jewish community withdrew their support of PUSH/Excel was that they saw their collective interests being threatened. The distinct possibility of that threat grew stronger as blacks gained more influence. They were willing to lend assistance as long as blacks did not present an economic threat to them, but when they saw a potentially strong competitor group arising, they reacted strongly.

How are the conflicts among these social groups adjudicated? Within the current social structure, one mechanism involves the official evaluation of social programs. Another is the use of standardized achievement test scores to allocate educational opportunities. However, the problem with the evaluation of PUSH/Excel was that the framework employed did not suit the type of effort PUSH/Excel was. The federal authorities did not intend the evaluation to be biased in this fashion. In fact, they intended the evaluation to be a stakeholder evaluation that would attend to the interests of the disadvantaged group to be served. However, the stakeholder aspects of the evaluation were quietly submerged, and quite a different evaluation framework was employed under the rubric of "stakeholder" evaluation. If one is to employ adjudicating mechanisms, they must be fair and just; in my opinion, the PUSH/Excel evaluation was not. This was a case in which the well-intended and well-motivated federal advocacy for the disadvantaged went awry, and it is often the case that federal actions initiated with the best of intentions to help the disadvantaged turn out to be subtly biased against them.

Thus many of the happenings in the PUSH/Excel saga can be understood as having social class conflict as their basis. The remaining questions about Jackson and PUSH/Excel can be more meaningfully addressed when viewed in the context of the long social history of

American race relations, of which these events are only the most recent part.

From Caste to Class

The Antebellum Preindustrial Period

William Julius Wilson (1980) has provided a historical view of the class basis of American race relations. He divides the history of race relations into three periods: the antebellum preindustrial period; the industrialization period; and the post–World War II period. The antebellum South was dominated by a small elite group of slaveholding whites who controlled not only the economy of the South but the politics as well. Their relationship with their black slaves was paternalistic rather than competitive, and part of this paternalism included protecting blacks from hostile working-class whites. This slave-owning aristocracy was not only able to impose its will on the slaves but also on three-quarters of the white population. The working-class whites were powerless. For their part the slaves were allowed their religion, and in this they developed a sense of identity and a limited form of resistance.

Where they could, working-class whites tried to restrict the rights of blacks, as competitive black workers took jobs and drove down wages. With the influx of 5 million Europeans into the country between 1830 and 1860, competition over jobs became more intense between whites and free blacks, especially for the Irish and other immigrants who settled in the large cities. Meanwhile, the states of the old Northwest Territory, especially Illinois, Indiana, and Ohio, were settled by nonslaveholding whites from the upper South, who migrated in large numbers to escape the domination of the southern plantation slaveholders. These whites had suffered from competition with slaves and free blacks alike; they moved vigorously both to prevent the expansion of slavery into the region and also to impose discriminatory barriers against blacks to prevent them from competing for jobs. These working-class whites were strongly antislavery yet strongly racist.

Once the blacks were freed after the Civil War, economic competition intensified as blacks came into direct competition with whites. With the weakening of the aristocratic planter class, white laborers in the South were able to gain some political power, much of which was directed at restricting blacks from competition. A new breed of southern politician emerged who combined the style of the southern preacher with racism. Huey Long and George Wallace are later well-known examples, and it might be noted that their populist rhetoric was based upon the evangelical style of the white Baptist church. These men had charisma for the white working class, much to the puzzlement of northerners, and for many of the same reasons that Jesse Jackson has charisma for blacks.

The Ku Klux Klan and Jim Crow segregation laws of the late nineteenth century were outgrowths of this brand of racism. Lynchings of blacks multiplied many times over during this period. The weakened southern white aristocracy supported the racist caste structure in order to insure the supply of low-wage labor, which they had acquired previously through slavery. Blacks were left with tenant farms in the South, where most blacks continued to live, marginal jobs that whites didn't want in the North, and no political power, at the bottom of a social caste system in which they were disdained.

The Industrialization Period

At the beginning of the industrialization period blacks in the North were limited to menial service jobs because of the surplus of immigrant workers from southern Europe at the turn of the century. The industrial jobs went to these new immigrants. However, immigration was sharply curtailed in about 1915, and blacks were then offered jobs in heavy industry to help the war effort. At the same time mechanization of southern agriculture was beginning to push southern black tenant farmers off the land, forcing them to migrate north for jobs. Millions of blacks migrated to the northern cities between 1940 and 1960. In 1890, 80 percent of the blacks were living in rural areas and 20 percent in cities; by 1970, 80 percent were in the cities and 20 percent in rural areas.

This migration north to the cities brought blacks into increasing job competition with whites. Blacks were often used by the industrialists as strike breakers; for example, in East St. Louis in 1916 and 1917, black strike breakers permanently replaced white workers in meatpacking jobs, and in Chicago in 1916–1921 and 1926, a similar process occurred. Large-scale race riots erupted in East St. Louis in 1917, where forty-eight people died, and in Chicago in 1919, where thirty-eight died. Even though blacks generally were relegated to the worst jobs in mills, foundries, and meatpacking, race relations remained tense, and these legacies of intense racism have endured.

The triangle of southern Illinois from East St. Louis south to Cairo also received a heavy in-migration of blacks from the South in the late nineteenth and early twentieth centuries—just what these whites had feared. The result was an intense racism among working-class whites directed at blacks that continues today. It was no surprise that this area later produced Martin Luther King's assassin, James Earl Ray—himself a product of the white industrial underclass of the region that is still imbued with racism based on the fear of economic competition with blacks (McMillan 1976).

The Post–World War II Period

White politicians managed this explosive racial antagonism by excluding blacks from the main political institutions. Excluded from political power, blacks did not have the means to care for their own needs and certainly were not cared for by the other groups. They therefore eventually registered their self-interest through the extrainstitutional activities of the civil rights movement. Only in the 1960s did blacks discover this way out of their predicament.

The urbanization and ghettoization of blacks had produced a black middle class that earned money mostly by providing services for the black community. It was this group that finally forged their deprived status into the civil rights movement, which was distinctly middle class in leadership, policies, and interests. In the preceding decades concentrated numbers of black voters in the largest cities finally gave blacks the votes to wrest political control of those cities away from the white ethnics who had controlled them for so many years, and blacks began to exert political influence in the big cities in the 1970s and 1980s. Blacks became competitive politically as well as economically, which increased racial tensions in cities like Chicago, Detroit, and Philadelphia.

However, just as blacks were beginning to take over some of the political machines in the large urban centers, these cities fell upon hard times. Because of radical changes in the national economy, the manufacturing jobs that had been the main support of these industrial cities ceased to expand and in fact contracted in many cases beginning in the 1960s. High-paying manufacturing jobs disappeared, which especially affected young black males, and the blacks inherited bankrupt cities with high unemployment rates (House and Madura 1987). The problem was not so much racial discrimination on the job or in unequal pay, but in the lack of high-paying blue-collar jobs altogether. City governments called upon to provide increasing city services did not have the resources to do so.

At the same time, job opportunities for the black middle class increased significantly, especially in the government. Affirmative action helped middle-class blacks substantially but helped working-class and underclass blacks much less. Middle-class blacks prospered and moved to the better neighborhoods, leaving the ghetto-bound underclass to struggle. A black person's social class now had as much to do with his or her life chances as race. Such is Wilson's historical overview of the interaction of race and class in American society, with a few elaborations.

Wilson's analysis suggests that racism in American is a legacy of slavery, economic exploitation, and competition. The underlying dynamics are contained in the interactions of the owner-planter-industrialist upper class, the black underclass, and the white working class, where virulent racist attitudes still persist. At the core of these interactions are relationships of economic domination, which translate into political domination. As various ethnic groups have immigrated into the country, they have used their collective ethnic identity to advance their economic interests. This view of American history sees the subjugation of blacks as central to the economic, political, and historical development of the United States itself and not simply a marginal aberration, as most interpretations would suggest. Hence, Americans have witnessed the resiliency of American racism in spite of universal condemnation.

The Black Middle Class

The emergence of a sizable black middle class implied considerable change for black politics, national politics, and American class dynamics. Between 1980 and 1985 the black middle class increased in size by 58 percent, compared to 4.3 percent for the white middle class, the white middle class already being much larger, of course. The expanding sector of government jobs accounted for a major portion of black middle-class employment. By 1986 40 percent of black households were officially classified as poor, 25 percent as working class, 29 percent as middle class, and 5 percent as upper class (Hill 1987).

The black middle class provided leadership for the civil rights movement, but the emergence of a large black middle class also portended new political problems for the black community and for black leadership. Some observers thought that a schism had been created within the black community, with an increasingly affluent middle class on the one side and an increasingly impoverished underclass on the other (Wilson 1980). Income inequality among blacks was already worse than income inequality among whites, and inequality among both groups increased during the 1980s (Brimmer 1987). The black middle class received 43.3 percent of all black income in 1985, compared to 36.1 percent in 1980. These figures show that the middle class was both getting larger and acquiring a larger proportion of black income—both numbers and money perhaps would be harbingers of political power. In the civil rights movement, this emerging black middle class focused on reforms that involved middle-class issues such as integrated public facilities and affirmative action. This political activity resulted in the expansion and prosperity of the middle class, but affirmative action did little good when there were no jobs to be found or when the only available jobs were so marginal that they could not support a family (Wilson 1980). Hence, a segmented labor market had developed that offered radically different opportunities to different classes of both blacks and whites.

PUSH/Excel and Class Structure

How did Jackson and PUSH/Excel fit into this changing class structure? PUSH/Excel was clearly an outgrowth of the civil rights movement and used similar tactics, although these tactics proved relatively ineffective in this case. PUSH/Excel itself was directed at black teenagers in the large urban ghetto high schools, some of whom were middle class but most of whom were underclass. Education had become even more important because the available jobs were increasingly tied to educational credentials (Landry 1987). Educational credentials were absolutely critical for blacks, even more so than for whites, if they were to secure good jobs. In fact, many black leaders and scholars contended that education was the *only* way out of the ghetto (Comer 1987). In the industrialization period education had not been necessary to obtain a reasonable livelihood, and in the antebellum period education had not been allowed for blacks. Jackson recognized that the high-paying factory jobs were disappearing and that the newly available jobs would be clerical, government, and service sector jobs that required a more extensive education. The schools were increasingly becoming the primary avenue of advancement for social and economic position.

The proper political and moral stance of the new black middle class caused anguish among its members. To what degree were they responsible for their unfortunate underclass brethren left behind? There was soul searching among this new class of blacks (Poussaint 1987; Frazier 1987; Hare 1987). These internal conflicts of the black middle class were embodied in PUSH/Excel in the person of Saundra Murray, the director of the AIR evaluation. She had strong aspirations to become the first black woman to conduct a prominent national evaluation (S. Murray 1982), and what better place to start than with PUSH/Excel? She became the director of the evaluation after it was under way, and she inherited the inappropriate evaluation framework designed by Charles Murray. The evaluation succeeded in describing the program but faltered in its ultimate assessments.

In her professional ambition Saundra Murray willingly embraced the role of the tough evaluator, following her image of how a professional evaluator should act. ("For the first three years that Excel was in existence, they got away with Hell. The funders didn't shoot straight about what was going on, and they didn't force the people to shape up. They need honest feedback and I plan to give it to them.") But she was torn by the conflict of having to declare the program a failure. At the same time, Jackson and his colleagues put tremendous pressure on her because she was black; some called her a traitor to her race. In my view, this was no place for a novice evaluator to be, especially one with divided loyalties. As shown in the interviews with Saundra Murray, the experience turned out to be a shattering one for her personally; she was a potential heroine put into a situation in which no heroic acts were possible. She was limited by the logic of the evaluation design and her professional aspirations on the one hand, but she also empathized with the youths the program was trying to help. These conflicts resulted in extreme personal anguish.

The larger question of conscience for the black middle class involved what social policies to pursue in the future. Should they pursue policies primarily for the black upper classes or for the lower classes? Some analysts contend that broad-based economic policies are the only way to sustain and help the poor and impoverished, that the old civil rights issues like affirmative action only helped the advantaged minorities. Thus, a new set of policies was necessary (Wilson 1987). Black leaders like Jackson had middle-class backgrounds, and his delegates to the 1984 Democratic convention were as well-off financially as those of his white opponents; they were drawn from the top financial portion of black society (Reed 1986). Furthermore, Jackson's main financial contributors, like entertainer Bill Cosby and Cadillac dealer Al Johnson, were wealthy indeed. The social policies the black leadership chose to pursue would not only affect black politics but would have a powerful impact on American social policy generally.

In summary, the fate of blacks has not been peripheral to the development of American society but has been in fact a central cog in the development of the American class structure, the dynamics of which involve the interactions of the governing upper class, the white working class, and the black underclass. One continuous element of this interaction has been racism. To put it another way, if Jesse Jackson saw himself as a producer of dramas for others to follow and the American schools as the theater for his PUSH/Excel drama, then the setting, the plot, and even some of the script were supplied by the dynamics of American class structure.

13

Jesse Jackson's Character

No matter what the accomplishments or failures of Jesse Jackson, most people continue to be fascinated by his character more than by anything else about him. This fascination explains Ralph Abernathy's pointed allusion that what is needed today is not *"charisma* so much as *character"* and two reporters' ambivalent reaction to Jackson as "intellectual dynamite . . . a bad black dude . . . our Savior . . . and a conniving, grandstanding Elmer Gantry" (Faw and Skelton 1986, 1). Black columnist Vernon Jarrett asserted that "[Jackson's] agenda is the promotion of Jesse Jackson as the King, the emperor, the most important black person of this century." It is almost impossible to discuss the man without someone volunteering strong opinions about his character.

The reason for this fascination, I believe, is that Jackson is a man of powerful internal contradictions. Internal contradiction, though, is what makes the United States one of the most fascinating countries in the world. The United States is the richest country in the world, yet has many homeless people walking its streets. As I see it, the United States is the world's best hope for democracy, yet it bullies its small neighbors. It has the most open government in the world, yet maintains a secret agency within the government unaccountable for its actions. It boasts equal opportunity for all, yet harbors a virulent racism. Which is the real United States? Such contradictions are what make for the fascination.

Jackson is similarly contradictory. Is he the selfless leader of an oppressed minority ready to put his life on the line, or is he a self-aggrandizing opportunist? Does he work for the poor and dispossessed, or does he make deals for the rich and powerful? Does he strive to make the voices of the meek heard, or does he crush dissent among his own followers? Which is he? What is his true identity? The truth, I believe, is that he is all of these things. He, too, is full of internal contradictions, and the content of his internal conflicts is peculiarly versus power, altruism versus self-aggrandizement, democracy versus effectiveness.

Most people base their opinion about Jackson's character entirely upon his personal qualities. But he is also a product of the historical events of his time, and the institutional forces are at least as influential as the personal ones. In assessing Jackson's character I would divide the issue into three parts—the difficulty of holding any charismatic leader accountable, the particular tradition of black leadership that has evolved over the past several centuries, and the background of Jackson's own personal development. These three phenomena come together to produce what we observe as his character.

Accountability and Charismatic Leadership

First, there is the question of how accountable any charismatic leader can be. Unless charismatic leaders hold political office or some other formal position, they are often not elected or selected by any procedure normally associated with political accountability, nor can they be dismissed by regular procedures. Even when they do hold political office, someone whose confidence is the "self-confidence linked to the conviction that one is destiny's child chosen to accomplish what others perceive as an impossible mission" are not likely to be bound by convention nor attend to the advice of others (Willner 1984, 146). Charismatic leaders have immense confidence in themselves and the rightness of their own positions, a confidence magnified by their followers' intense devotion. Jesse Jackson's self-confidence was gauged by one observer, Robert Tucker, who said that Jackson not only believes in God but firmly believes that God believes in him (Joyce 1983).

The accountability issue regarding Jackson has been raised most forcefully by Adolph L. Reed, Jr., in his book, *The Jesse Jackson Phenomenon* (1986). Charismatic leaders derive their authority as spokespersons from the constituency they are presumed to represent, but it is difficult to ascertain whether their leadership is truly authentic. The validation of a charismatic leader comes by acclamation rather than by election or selection. In the case of racial minorities, outsiders are forced to rely upon circumstantial evidence to judge whether the leadership is "racially authentic," and this judgment is no easy task. In other words, the leader's legitimacy as leader of his people is dependent upon judgments made outside the normal electoral or political processes.

A corollary of evaluating this kind of "organic" leadership is that it is usually assumed that all members of the minority have uniform attitudes and interests and that the leader represents those interests faithfully. There is no routine way for the presumed constituents to register their dissatisfactions and discontents; this limitation yields a situation in which the leader is distant from the constituency and not directly accountable to them. Under these conditions it is often assumed that the objectives of the leader represent the interests of the constituents, which may not be the case.

The Tradition of Black Leadership

Furthermore, debate and dissent within the minority community are often interpreted as disloyalty to the minority cause; consequently, the leadership that develops is often not based on a rational discussion of issues but on direction imposed by the leader. Minority charismatic leadership is often antidiscursive and antidemocratic and tends to be authoritarian. This tendency is further complicated by the fact that the traditional leaders of the black church have been authoritarian preachers certified by white elites.

> As Frazier indicated, "the pattern of control and organization of the Negro church has been authoritarian, with a strong man in a dominant position." The basis of clerical authority lies outside the temporal world and is not susceptible to secular dispute. The community constituted in the church is not reproduced through open discourse but is bound by consensual acceptance of a relation that vests collective judgment in the charismatic authority of the minister. . . . The model of authority is fundamentally antiparticipatory and antidemocratic; in fact, it is grounded on a denial of the rationality that democratic participation requires (Reed 1986, 56–57).

Under these conditions leaders tend to embody and display collective values rather than to construct policy agencies that will serve the material interests of the group, to be symbolic at the expense of being instrumentally effective. For example, the leader of the National Baptist Convention, J. H. Jackson, endorsed Ronald Reagan for the presidency in 1980 (Reed 1986), whom most blacks strongly opposed, and his predecessor vehemently opposed Martin Luther King's campaign to challenge the Daley machine in Chicago. In fact, the longtime collaboration of black church ministers with the white governing elites, no doubt through historical necessity, has often resulted in political agendas in which the interests of many blacks were not addressed; in fact, it has led to situations in which ministerial influence was too often traded for self-interest (Reed 1986). Within the constraints of such leadership, black political activity has sometimes become no more than an expressive catharsis without benefiting the interests of those it would serve.

Jesse Jackson was a product of these historical forces. He conceived of himself as the producer of dramas for others to follow. In fact, he was an actor in dramas produced by many other people and the scripts were embedded in the institutions of his country, past and present. His leadership grew out of the civil rights movement, complete with its religious and middle-class foundations. This southern tradition called for a particular oratory and leadership style because that was the type of leadership blacks had been allowed to develop; it also called for working with white elites and reaching bargains and compromises with them. Jackson was enormously successful in dealing with white business leaders and politicians, running into difficulty only when he led black interests against the interests of other socioeconomic groups.

The southern charismatic tradition also called for accepting favors for one's services and living well, for being divinely inspired and inwardly directed, sometimes contrary to other advice. This tradition also made for compromised leaders and for the white stereotype of black ministers and politicians. Black leaders were both compromising and compromised; the two characteristics went hand in hand. The tradition called for authoritative if not authoritarian command of one's followers, and it also called for personal sacrifice if necessary to advance the opportunities of one's people while not closing down on one's own opportunities.

Jackson was far better able to deal with the southern hierarchical power structure in Chattanooga, and they with him, than with the more pluralistic, open, and competitive power structures in the northern and western cities. He understood the southern power elites and they understood him; he knew what was possible and what was not possible. In general, it is not as easy to make private deals with school leaders as it is to do so with corporation heads because the schools are more open to public inspection and more vulnerable to the demands of a number of interest groups. Jackson's deals with businesses could be conducted in secrecy through private bargaining with white elites. Thus, he was most successful in PUSH/Excel when he could deal with the southern white elites.

Jackson became susceptible to questions of proper accountability because he had arisen to power through the involvement of important segments of the white-controlled media. Some of his most virulent critics charged that he was too much the creation of the white media, which could not detect the difference between a genuine mass movement and a "group of people shouting in a church" (Reed 1986, 12). Dealing with white corporations had helped wealthier blacks, critics claimed, but not the poor. In his 1984 presidential endeavor, he did not develop an agenda of specific issues until late in the campaign, preferring instead to emphasize traditional black symbolism. Some analysts claimed that he still had not addressed the real concerns of poor black people. But, to be fair, the media did not always concentrate on the content of his issues, focusing instead on his performance.

Charismatic leaders generally operate outside the normal political processes and often cannot be held accountable in traditional ways. Black leaders and ministers have had their own particular difficulties. Financial control of operations has been one of Jackson's worst problems. In January 1985 he flew back from Europe on the Concorde with four of his children and several aides at a cost of $2,000 per person when many of his staff had not been paid for three weeks (Faw and Skelton 1986). Jackson's personal finances were scrutinized in an article in the *Washington Post* April 10, 1988 (Babcock 1988). But some of these flaws are also true of noncharismatic white politicians, not to mention fundamentalist preachers. Incidents like these, including the Martin Luther King blood-on-the-shirt episode, as well as genuine care and concern for the poor and the dispossessed, show Jackson's character in all its contradictions.

Jackson's Personal Characteristics

Finally, there are Jackson's unique personal characteristics. As I have already described, Jackson was raised in disreputable status as an illegitimate son and known to the community as such. His background apparently gave him an insatiable appetite for media attention and for gaining the respect he felt lacking for himself personally and for blacks in general. He cast social issues in personal terms, unable sometimes to detect the difference between what was important for him and what was important for his constituency, a serious flaw which gave adversaries too much advantage since they could meet the personal demands of a few people far more cheaply than the welfare of a vast constituency. He once said, "The bottom line is my self-respect, that is what they must come to terms with" (Faw and Skelton 1986).

These characteristics and his position as the preeminent leader of the black minority made Jackson one of the most controversial people in American and one of the most fascinating. How can one judge Jackson's character given these contradictions? Should one simply write him off as being fundamentally flawed, as many of his critics have done? Or should one excuse his flaws because he is black and because blacks have had such an excruciating ordeal in this country? What standards should one employ in judging black leaders such as Jackson?

Jackson's Accountability

There are two common approaches to judging black politics and politicians (Reed 1986). One approach sees black politics as totally different from mainstream politics. Therefore the same rules and standards need not apply. There is a tendency among many liberals taking this view to romanticize blacks as representing a more "authentic" humanity and hence to excuse them from critical judgment altogether. The other approach is to treat black politics as merely an extreme case of ethnic group politics and thus to overlook its own intrinsically important features. Although the two approaches seem fundamentally opposed to one another, they both result in not examining black politics in a serious, critical manner. "In both cases exceptionalist assumptions separate explanation of black politics from a need to examine endemic characteristics—such as patterns of cleavage, nature of political argument, and styles of legitimation—that mediate the black community's structural integration into the polity" (Reed 1986, 118). The time has indeed come to judge black leaders against the same standards as leaders of other groups.

The ultimate question of accountability then was not whether Jackson wore expensive suits or had a six-figure income. Almost all nationally prominent American politicians had that. Having the personal qualities of an ascetic may make one a better person but it does little for one's accountability. The critical accountability issue was whether Jackson truly represented the interests of the poor and dispossessed as he claimed to do and as he no doubt wanted to do. That was the ultimate criterion, just as the ultimate question of accountability for the United States as the most powerful country in the world, I believe, is not its lifestyle but the degree to which it as a society provides for its own poor and dispossessed and the degree to which as a nation it offers leadership to the rest of the world in improving conditions for all who lived in it. The answers to both questions involve controversy and internal contradiction.

There is no doubt about Jackson's rhetoric but his actions are not so clear. There are several distinct possibilities as to whose interests he might represent. First, he might represent all blacks, but only blacks. In this view, the poor have no special claim upon his leadership. In the not too distant past, representing the interests of blacks and the poor were one and the same thing because almost all blacks were poor. But this situation changed dramatically within Jackson's lifetime with the emergence of a black middle class and even traces of a black upper class. One could still support blacks generally, but the same social agenda would not serve all blacks to an equal degree. So there was possibly a choice to be made between blacks generally and the black poor.

There was also possibly a choice to be made as to whether to represent blacks exclusively or to represent the poor of all colors—the Rainbow Coalition. Jackson was one of the first black leaders to face this choice, for few American blacks had ever had the opportunity to represent interests that went beyond those of their race. Up to now Jackson had always chosen to "run black" when it came down to it, and of course, the choice of representing a multiracial constituency might well be an illusion because whites might never follow a black leader. Racism and racial politics are still alive and well. Before the 1984 and 1988 presidential campaigns, it was not clear what would happen if Jackson tried to represent a multiracial constituency because such a thing had not been attempted at a national level. Representing the interests of the widest group of poor people was the noblest possible goal for Jackson; representing his own interests was the least noble.

On the one hand, there was no politician in America who more frequently expressed concern for the poor and the dispossessed and did it so eloquently as Jackson. His speech at the 1984 Democratic Convention was a masterpiece in this regard. It was a paean to national unity required for any serious presidential candidate and in addition an analysis of the ills and deprivations visited upon the poor of all colors in the United States. And it elicited tremendous positive emotional response from the whites.

But it angered Jackson's black followers in the convention hall—and here was one of the most difficult problems. To represent the interests of the poor and dispossessed of all colors required pulling away from an exclusively black agenda and possibly from a black middle-class agenda as well. Constructing an instrumental policy agenda for helping the poor regardless of color meant giving up or at least moderating the charismatic relationship Jackson had with his followers. Not only would this strategy involve the risk of losing black followers, it also meant sacrificing the intense personal satisfaction that came from being adored by his people as a demigod among them, and that was a lot to lose.

In a sense charismatic leaders must be captives of their own followers even as they captivate their followers. For if the followers need charisma and charismatic leaders to give them a clear identity in the moral world, how much more so do the leaders need their followers to complete themselves and to give them an important place in that world? This mutual dependency would be true of any charismatic leader but surely it would be intensified for a man needing personal respect and recognition the way Jackson did. Jackson's personal traits suggest that he might not be able to give up his charismatic style and constituency.

Although there was never any question about Jackson's personal courage or his physical, intellectual, and political abilities, his need for respect and adoration, I think, locked him into a particular expressive relationship with his followers in which he was both captor and captive and from which he clearly derived immense satisfaction. To pursue other, more instrumental objectives for a larger constituency was to risk all— to risk his constituency and thus leadership itself. Frankly, I do not know which path he will pursue, although his critics within the black community had already arrived at a less than ennobling answer.

But such an answer is too simple, just as it is too simple to declare that the United States is simply one more imperial power and dismiss its future accordingly. Such an answer does not grasp the complete nature of the internal contradictions of the United States itself. There is a good side as well as a bad side, and it is possible for the United States to struggle for its better side, to lead its better side over its worse side. Similarly, it is possible that Jesse Jackson will work out his own internal contradictions in such a way that his better self wins, even if it means overcoming tradition, childhood scars, and institutional structures. Most great leaders have struggled with themselves and won. Jackson himself said that character should be measured by how we treat the destitute. It is possible that he will yet prove himself as a great leader of all America as well as a great leader for American blacks.

As for Jackson's effort to save the black teenagers of his country, PUSH/Excel had failed. And it was already slipping into the realm of history, reconstruction, and myth:

> Perhaps the most lasting legacy of charismatic political leadership is the postmortem charismatic myth in which it becomes clothed. As has been noted, the charismatic leader gains his charisma in part through tapping the traditional myths and symbols of his society. Subsequently, he and his works take on in turn a mythic quality and become part of the reservoir of myths and symbols of that society and perhaps even for others. He and his deeds are then drawn upon by the leaders and generations that follow. Even those for whom he was not charismatic and those for whom he ceased being so did share in the drama he enacted. And they too transmit its awe and aura to their descendants. The image of a past and even of a defeated charismatic leader may serve as a standard of measure against which those who succeed him are viewed (Willner 1984, 199).

The main reason why Jesse Jackson's PUSH for Excellence had failed was that other socioeconomic groups in America were pushing in the opposite direction. Sometimes Jackson was pushing in other directions as well; it remained to be seen how far Jesse Jackson himself would progress in his own personal push for excellence.

14

Postscript: The Presidential Campaigns

As PUSH/Excel faded from the national limelight, Jesse Jackson became an even more prominent public figure in the United States: He put PUSH/Excel behind him and became a presidential candidate. Jackson took a leave from Operation PUSH to pursue the presidency in 1984 and then resigned altogether. Several successive heads of PUSH came and went, one being the Reverend Hycel B. Taylor, who resigned in 1986 after only seven months, saying, "No organization can succeed on the coattails or the charisma of one leader" (Overbea 1986). Reverend Willie T. Barrow then reassumed the office.

By 1987 the federal audits of PUSH/Excel still had not been resolved. Of the $4.9 million in federal funds awarded to PUSH/Excel, the government claimed that the organization would have to repay more than $1 million because of a lack of documentation as to how the funds had been spent. This sum included $671,000 to the Department of Education, plus interest; $557,000 to the Department of Labor; and $38,642 to the Department of Commerce. Government officials had threatened to turn the case over to the Justice Department for legal action. Sharon Robinson, the national director, said that PUSH/Excel was trying to reach a repayment agreement with the government and to continue its work. PUSH/Excel struggled along at a greatly diminished pace without fanfare (Burton 1987).

Meanwhile, Jackson himself launched a full-scale bid for the presidency—an endeavor amazingly similar to PUSH/Excel in many ways. Of course, his charisma was now exercised not in a predominantly black society but in a society 90 percent white. Although with 25 million blacks America has a larger black population than most nations, the larger society is still dominated by 200 million whites. This fact very much shaped and limited the influence of Jackson's charismatic appeal.

Many whites had an intensely negative reaction to Jackson, and this backlash was far more visible in his presidential campaign than in PUSH/Excel.

Before the 1960s, it was assumed in white America that minority groups like blacks would have their own leaders, and when it was important to know what blacks thought about an issue, one could consult those leaders, just as one would consult the heads of the labor unions about labor issues. It was not expected that black leaders would comment on national policies that did not directly affect blacks. Such influence was reserved for majority politicians. When Martin Luther King finally spoke out against the Vietnam War, he lost support from Lyndon Johnson and large segments of the white public, even though disproportionate numbers of young blacks were dying there. For example, *Newsweek* accused King of "simplistic political judgment" and of favoring a country "in which a race conscious minority dictated foreign policy" (Oates 1982, 437). The *New York Times* suggested that King's leadership should be directed toward the ghettos, not Vietnam. Other media reactions were similar. Black leaders were expected to keep their place and not comment on wider social issues.

Jackson's Image

The primary sources of Jackson's authority did not carry over to the white population, and the emotionalism displayed in the PUSH meetings and in the black churches was also foreign to most whites. In fact, many whites perhaps found it a little frightening. They saw Jackson excite large crowds and they heard slogans used to stunning effect. They not only did not like such emotionalism being incited in the black community, they also did not like the messages he conveyed. They approved of Jackson's exhortations to black teenagers to work hard, to study, to stay off drugs, and to get ahead. They thought that blacks needed self-discipline and besides, such issues were black concerns; the black leader was speaking to black teenagers. But when Jackson excited crowds with slogans like "From the outhouse to the White House!" and "We want it all!" and "Our time has come!" the whites were uneasy. These slogans dealt with national politics. Jackson was inciting emotional crowds of blacks to seize power, some thought, and many whites who felt that they themselves were the targets of this drive felt threatened. The large black minority was stirring, and the most visible instigator was Jesse Jackson.

Martin Luther King had done everything within his ability to appear nonthreatening to whites. The cornerstone of his nonviolent philosophy was to appeal to the consciences of whites; he thought that arousing their fears would get in the way of reaching that objective. Although always espousing a nonviolent strategy, Jackson clearly did not worry so much about being perceived as a threat, and many blacks admired him for saying things without regard for white reaction.

Jackson's first foray into presidential politics got him onto the covers of the news magazines, and their portrayal of him reflected his image in the larger society. In a cover story shortly before his presidential candidacy was announced, *Time* (Isaacson 1983) characterized Jackson as a Tom Paine, a Pied Piper, and a nonviolent guerrilla fighter whose magnetic gifts "generated excitement" and "created fervor." According to the article, Jackson was also self-promoting, showy, and flashy, a pitchman and a hustler and with this combination might "create a groundswell of support," "reshape the political landscape," "provoke intense hatred," and "injure the black cause"—a frightening prospect for the white establishment.

Newsweek (Morganthau et al. 1983) saw him as a "black messiah," a "champion," a "mesmerizing power." He was portrayed as a workaholic, a perfectionist, a striver filled with passion and energy who was hyperaggressive, self-proclaimed, and defiantly self-assertive. In addition to characterizing Jackson as potent and provocative, the magazine also described him as an opportunist, a flimflam man and called him erratic, reckless, unorthodox. He was also disorganized, unprepared, dilatory, more talk than action. He was capable, the article said, of setting off a white backlash, raising black expectations too high, and of splitting black voters. He was ultimately seen as a disruptive force.

As his campaign picked up steam, *U.S. News and World Report* reporters (Thornton and Mashek 1983) portrayed him as a threat, a force to be reckoned with. In their words, through his "spellbinding, high-voltage oratory," he "captured audiences," "hypnotized crowds," and "electrified blacks." His relentless drive and ruthless character made him seem somewhat "demonic." Combined with his arrogance and unpredictability, the threat was clear: In the view of the reporters he was likely to alarm whites, frustrate blacks, shake up the election, and split the Democratic party.

All of these articles used the following words to portray Jackson's opponents: fretting, sweating, appalled, cautious, ambivalent, wary, disapproving, grudging, resentful, and petrified. In short, they seemed to be helpless before his powerful onslaught—a curious way of casting a minority candidate with almost no chance of winning. Other words used to characterize Jackson in two of the articles were *spellbinding, relentless, ruthless, unpredictable, arrogant,* and *a threat.* The news magazines were in agreement about Jackson's charismatic power, which they saw as "spellbinding," an "electric power at his disposal." Combined with his relentless drive, fierce energy, and aggressiveness, he was a force to be reckoned with. In addition, his perceived ruthlessness and unpredictability made him a threat—perhaps even a dangerous one in the view of the media. The overall picture from the news magazines was of a somewhat satanic, definitely threatening figure.

What he threatened to do was to raise black expectations too high, set off a white backlash, divide Democrats as well as blacks, create a groundswell, and reshape electoral politics permanently, in short, to disrupt the political order. In the view of the mass media two other qualities lessened this threat. One was his reputation as a self-seeking hustler, which meant that he was only out for himself and perhaps not a serious revolutionary after all. Second, his reputation as a disorganized leader with more talk than action, a perception based upon PUSH/Excel as much as anything, made him appear less effective. But for the most part he was perceived as a serious threat, and it was precisely his perceived effectiveness that made him threatening and that aroused strong negative emotions, not his perceived lack of it.

In contrast, an article in *Black Enterprise* (Brown 1983) described Jackson as a "maverick," a "gadfly," and a "manipulator of the media." He was a popular and independent leader who was building a crusade, inspiring masses of people, raising concerns, aggressively attacking the political parties, and hoping to be in a position to bargain and exact concessions. He was "long on charisma" and "short on organizational skills and follow-through." The entire article was more detached, more objective, and less emotional than the national news magazines. The black media were not threatened.

A Black President

To understand either a prophet or a revolutionary leader fully, one must understand the symbols of power in the particular culture. Every political order has a governing elite and a set of symbolic forms that express the fact that the elite is in fact governing (Geertz 1983, 143). These symbols include myths, legends, stories, images, ceremonies, and rituals that indicate to the populace that things are as they should be, that the government is legitimate. In the words of an anthropologist, "A world wholly demystified is a world wholly depoliticized" (Geertz 1983, 143). Political orders live by their symbols as much as by their laws, and even a prophet or revolutionary leader must play off these cultural forms to be effective, as in fact the Ayatollah Khomeini successfully did against the Shah of Iran.

No central symbol captures the political faith of Americans as does the presidency (Robertson 1980). The presidency is seen by Americans as being the most powerful position in the world. To them the president literally has earth-shaking and potentially earth-destroying powers; the presidency is the center of all power and as such is an awe-inspiring office. The myth requires that the president be decisive, active, visible, and mobile, and this image is enhanced when the president moves around constantly—traveling, jetting across the country, helicoptering to Camp David. Much daily media coverage is devoted to the sheer physical movements of the president.

Above all, the president must be seen as being effective, as being the ultimate problem-solver, manager of crises, policy-maker, and program initiator. One of the worst things the president can do is to appear ineffective, as Jimmy Carter did in his attempts to free the American hostages in Iran. As Americans have felt a lessening of control over events that shape their lives, they have intensified their belief in the president's power to control events. National and international crises can be solved by presidential action, they believe, or at least they would like to believe.

In the public mind, the great mission of the president is to unify the country, including his own party, his administration, and the nation as a whole, because if the country is unified nothing can defeat it or impede its collective will. According to the prevailing myth, America is constantly threatened by crises of fragmentation and diversity. The president is the symbol and chief agent of national unity, the one person who represents the interests of all the people. By contrast, Congress represents local constituencies and special interests and is often ineffective, inefficient, bumbling, short-sighted, even corrupt, in the popular image (Robertson 1980).

To personify the national interest, the president must be idealistic, eloquent, just, and efficient. The perfect example is Abraham Lincoln, a humble man of the people, a moral leader, an emancipator, a war-time commander, and above all one who preserved the unity of the nation at its most divisive time. The popular belief is that even if the president does not possess these virtues in advance, the office itself will ennoble him and elevate his character. The most disturbing thing about the Watergate crisis was that Nixon was less than noble; he contradicted the myth of the presidency. An individual may be weak but not while serving as president. The president should be powerful, decisive, and independent, a John Wayne individualist who acts in the country's best interest. To fulfill the great mission of creating an integrated, unified country, the president also needs access to the mass media and must use it well.

How well did Jesse Jackson's public image measure up to this myth? In the mass media Jackson was portrayed as active, mobile, and decisive as he made grand entrances to major cities and associated with world leaders. He was eloquent, persuasive, and a master of the media. All these traits fit the image of the presidency well. On the other hand, he was portrayed as being self seeking and arrogant as opposed to idealistic and humble. His effectiveness and managerial ability were also questioned.

But the major liability of Jackson's image in 1984 was that he was perceived as being divisive. The president is supposed to unify the nation and prevent fragmentation. As the leader of the largest minority group, Jackson made demands of the establishment that whites saw as disruptive to national unity. Minority leaders are normally seen as being divisive because they threaten the status quo. So, racism aside, any minority leader would have an image problem in a quest for the presidency. Jackson's difficult task was to demonstrate somehow an ability to unify the country. His charisma alone is not likely to carry over to the majority white population because charisma is particular to the group in which it is exercised, as evidenced in the 1984 presidential campaign.

The 1984 Presidential Campaign

After Harold Washington's bitter, hard-fought mayoral campaign in Chicago, which climaxed in victory on February 22, 1983, and in which Jackson was portrayed as being "selfish, cocky, rash, and militant—with only his true interests at heart," Jesse Jackson began thinking about running for the presidency of the United States (Majors 1983, 10). Two reporters from CBS News followed Jackson throughout his 1984 campaign and detailed events in a book entitled *Thunder in America*, "Thunder" being the code name the Secret Service gave him (Faw and Skelton 1986). Jackson's presidential campaign mirrored his PUSH/Excel crusade to a remarkable extent.

Throughout the summer of 1983 he crisscrossed the south, visiting churches and giving speeches, building suspense as to whether he would run.

"Run, and you can win your self-respect. If you run, you may lose. But if you don't run, you're guaranteed to lose," he would tell them.

"Run, run, run," they would cry.

"From welfare to our share . . . from the slave ship to championship. . . . Hands that once picked cotton can now pick presidents," he would cry.

"Run, Jesse, run," their chant would rock the hall.

"Weeping may endure for a night, but joy will be coming in the morning. Suffering breeds character, character breeds faith, and in the end faith will not disappoint. Our time has come. *Our time has come. Our time—has come.*"

The crowd would be on its feet as the speaker sagged back on the stage, his clothes bathed in sweat—and the mighty voice would shout in unison: "Run, Jesse, run."

Electrifying: no other word describes that 1983 southern crusade. Jackson preached passion and the congregations caught fire (Faw and Skelton 1986, 30).

On August 30, the twentieth anniversary of Martin Luther King's famous "I Have a Dream" March on Washington, the crusade climaxed with a massive rally at the Lincoln Memorial. Jackson stood in front of the white-marbled monument:

But around him blacks and whites in the crowd, men and women, were smiling, jubilant, some almost delirious. They want things to change, they wanted a candidate—and they wanted it now. Slowly the cadence swept over the assembled. "Run, Jesse, run," the voices began, and as the preacher spoke, the chants continued, growing louder with each wave until the crowd was roaring, shouting the phrase again and again. "Run, Jesse, run" (Faw and Skelton 1986, 15–16).

After several months' buildup, Jackson announced his candidacy on "60 Minutes" before a television audience of 40 million people. This time the reporter was Mike Wallace instead of Dan Rather. Jackson was the last candidate to join the race and his early campaign was disorganized. Although the crowds were large and enthusiastic, his campaign manager, Arnold Pinkney, said, "Oh my god, what a mess" (Faw and Skelton 1986, 34). The National Baptist Convention, with 7 million black members, lent its strong support, and Jackson decided to concentrate his campaign in states with large black populations, especially in the South. His campaign was directed toward black audiences, and observers commented that he had to "run black." Running black, however, did not enhance his image with whites.

On December 8, 1983, Lt. Robert Goodman was shot down in a combat mission and captured by the Syrians. The Reagan administration made no progress in obtaining his release, so Jackson once again prepared a Middle East trip, this time to rescue Goodman. The trip was condemned by the Reagan administration and the media; before he left, Jackson called the producer of "60 Minutes" for media advice, who advised him to take along a prominent white clergyman. None was available; instead, Jackson took Louis Farrakhan, leader of the black Muslims, who proved valuable with his religious affiliation and knowledge of Arabic. After a two-hour meeting with President Assad, Goodman was released, and Jackson and Goodman returned to the United States triumphant and appeared together on talk shows. Although some claimed the whole episode was grandstanding, most observers were impressed, and his campaign gained momentum.

Then on January 25, 1984, in a conversation with a black reporter, Jackson referred to New York City as "Hymietown" and to New York Jews as "Hymie," thus creating a national furor directed at himself once again. Again he became defensive, denying culpability and claiming there was a Jewish conspiracy to destroy him. The media lambasted him, his money dwindled, and within a few weeks his campaign was on the verge of collapse, just as PUSH for Excellence had deteriorated in the aftermath of the Middle East trip in 1979. Seeing Jackson under attack, many American blacks expressed anger toward Jews for creating the situation and for other suppressed grievances.

Jackson had already been the subject of strong Jewish opposition. An advertisement soliciting money for the defeat of his presidential candidacy, sponsored by the Jews Against Jackson committee founded by Rabbi Meier Kahane, had appeared in the *New York Times* on November 11, 1983. The ad displayed the photo of Jackson embracing Arafat in 1979 and asked, "Do You Believe Any Jew Should Support This Man? Should *Any* Decent American?" Hostilities between blacks and Jews intensified dramatically. Reluctantly, under intense pressure, Jackson apologized for his remarks, but the controversy continued.

Underlying the enmity toward Jackson was his stand on the Middle East. Rabbi David Saperstein, who had tried to mediate between Jackson and Jewish groups, said, "For Jews, Jackson was the archetypal foe of Israel, the friend of Arafat, the champion of the PLO. That for them was all that mattered. That was all they could see. Nothing else. They were blind to anything else. On the other hand, most blacks could care less about the Middle East. For them, Jackson was a symbol of their aspirations, that was the extent of their perceptions—that was all that counted for them. They too were blind" (Faw and Skelton 1986, 76). Rabbi Stephen Weiss said, "Israel colors every relationship that Jews have with every group or force; as an item it has poisoned Christian-Jewish relations. . . . Israel colors everything, damn it. Jews want to know where a guy is on Israel, first and foremost" (Faw and Skelton 1986, 67). Jackson was the only major presidential candidate who supported negotiations with the Palestinians.

But the problem ran even deeper than the PLO issue. According to public opinion polls blacks were more anti-Semitic than other groups. Blacks felt they had been exploited historically by Jews who had been landlords, merchants, lawyers, and teachers. In affirmative action and quota cases, such as the Bakke case, blacks found Jewish organizations in opposition to black interests. There was strong animosity between Jews and blacks *within* the American setting. The backlash against

Jackson enveloped Jews as well as other whites. Al Vorspan, of the Union of American Hebrew Congregations, said: "Nobody wanted to admit that when Jesse Jackson gets up there on network television, and there are ninety million people out there watching, and he says 'Our time has come, Our time has come'—nobody wants to say 'fuck you, Jackson, your time has not come.' But that's what they're thinking. Because if *your* time has come, then what has happened to *my* time" (Faw and Skelton 1986, 39).

And, of course, the backlash against Jackson extended far beyond the Jewish community. A white service station owner in Louisiana said, "We've subsidized laziness so damn much that where's the work ethic anymore? . . . Hell, the formula is to go out there and *make* your damn money and quit your bitchin.' . . . Jackson? We have *arriiiiiived.* Our time has *cooooome.* . . . Well, Hell, his time has always been here, same as mine has. Get out there and work for it" (Faw and Skelton 1986, 26). A white architect from North Carolina said, "If he was white, everybody would be for him . . . another James Jones, if you will. They can lead you to death if you don't watch it" (p. 148). Or a white cab driver in the PUSH/Excel town of Chattanooga: "Never heard of no Jesse Jackson. Just heard of some nigger running around making a lot of noise" (p. 215).

The campaign sputtered on. Reporters with the Jackson entourage complained that logistically it was the most inept campaign of all time. When they arrived at towns, there was sometimes no transportation waiting, no reservations for lodging, and no telephones for the reporters to file deadlines. Jackson called all the shots, making all the decisions about where the campaign was going each day and personally approving each appearance, often adding stops at the spur of the moment (Faw and Skelton 1986, 97). When reporters complained about this lack of organization, Jackson rejoined that they were accustomed to too many luxuries, the product of a soft upbringing.

He drew almost entirely black crowds, using his pithy slogans and rhymes. Whites stayed away from these gatherings. Bishop H. H. Brookins, an advisor, said, "Jesse frightened people. . . . The way he came across to the white person . . . he was intimidating. I'm saying that many of the non-black people saw Jesse as an anathema. See, he registered something in them. He sparked something in them that turned them off" (Faw and Skelton 1986, 98).

On the other hand, blacks were very much "turned on." As a black couple walked away from a rally in New Jersey, the man said, "That man got a lot of nerve." The woman responded, "If he don't be a winner, he sure give them a fright" (Faw and Skelton 1986, 5). And he did frighten the whites, so much so that he received more than 300 death threats, more than all the other candidates combined, and eleven suspects were reportedly arrested. Geraldine Ferraro, the Democratic vice presidential candidate, said, "It was something around him you could almost feel. I've been on stage with [Senator Edward] Kennedy lots of times too, and he's always a target, but that was nothing like this. This was just a feeling that something was imminent, something menacing" (Faw and Skelton 1986, 101). She instructed her three children not to stand near him.

When Jackson came under attack for his Hymietown remark, Black Muslim leader Louis Farrakhan came to his "aid," calling Judaism a "dirty religion," Hitler "a great man," and threatening "to punish with death" the black reporter who had revealed the remarks. Whites, particularly Jews, called upon Jackson to repudiate Farrakhan. Jackson refused to do so, further alienating the whites. Jackson's advisors felt that if he repudiated Farrakhan directly he would lose black support because Farrakhan expressed the anger that many blacks also felt.

During the early primaries in the south, Jackson did not do as well as he had hoped but he did well enough, largely through the black vote, to remain among the three Democratic contenders finishing the race. More and more, he turned to the black churches for his support. In most states he finished second or third, and in all the primaries no more than 9 percent of his vote had been white, while he captured 70 or 80 percent of the black vote. "The way Jackson told it, how one voted was a new way to measure one's blackness, a new way to affirm membership in the black community. It was, said his critics, the 'politics of race'" (Faw and Skelton 1986, 129).

By the time the Democratic Convention was held in San Francisco Jackson had amassed 3.5 million primary votes and 384 pledged delegates, quite a respectable showing, although not enough to determine planks in the Democratic platform or to influence the vice presidential nomination. However, his affirmative action policy was adopted, and he was selected to give one of the main speeches at the convention. For two weeks before the event he gave inconsistent signals as to what he would say, raising concern about how conciliatory and supportive he would be. The Democratic leadership worried and wondered. Then, with 33 million Americans watching on television, the largest audience for any speaker at either convention, Jackson delivered his speech. And given the place and circumstances, it was brilliant. Only this time, it was the whites who were crying, while the blacks sat silent and angry.

When the election was finished, the reactions to Jackson's campaign were as mixed as the reactions to PUSH/Excel. Black voter registration was up by 1.2 million in eleven southern states, nearly 30 percent over the 1980 election. More blacks and a higher percentage of blacks voted in primaries and caucuses than ever before, and an additional 740,000 blacks voted in the general election in November. Observers pointed out that many other factors had contributed to the enormous black turnout, but most agreed that Jackson had had a tremendous mobilizing effect. Some thought the main benefit of the campaign was not the increased vote count but the psychological feeling among blacks that they could be more politically assertive.

Other observers, such as William Schneider of the conservative American Enterprise Institute, thought that Jackson was a "poisonous influence" because he polarized people (Faw and Skelton 1986, 213). Many whites felt that blacks had gone too far, that whites had become the targets of black hostility directed at them. One white supporter who had been at the rally at the Lincoln Memorial said "I felt left out. . . . I got the sense that without openly courting the hostility that blacks feel toward whites he implicitly tried to exploit it and take advantage of it. . . . It's hard to specify it more than that. I just sensed the kind of meanness I didn't like" (Faw and Skelton 1986, 218–219). In the five southern states where 400,000 blacks had been added to the registration lists, *white* registration had increased by 1.2 million, and many of those were whites who voted Republican in the general election; presumably, they registered so they could vote against Jackson's candidacy. Jesse Jackson himself said, "The bottom line is my self-respect; that is what they must come to terms with" (p. 246).

The 1984 Convention Speech

Why did Jackson's speech to the 1984 Democratic Convention bring the whites to tears and the blacks to anger? After their respectable showing in the primaries, his supporters at the convention were given few concessions by the Democratic Party, and they were angered by this rebuff. They waited for Jackson to lambast the white leaders of the Party in his speech. The whites, for their part, must have feared strong words of retribution from Jackson.

Many of Jackson's black supporters were extremely disappointed in the actual speech, thinking it far too conciliatory:

I thought it was bullshit. . . . Gradually I'm realizing that white people around me are crying. I mean the men. I'm not talking about no lightweight little white girls. I'm talking about we're-going-to-fight-you-nigger-till-you-gone white folks. They were sitting in tears . . . [and] this white lady from Mississippi . . . there in tears on my shoulder. I realized my God, I'm part of something very important. . . . I don't think any of us were prepared to sit there and watch those white men and women from Mississippi sit there, in tears. I mean, we don't touch each other. . . . Well goddam, I thought, where am I?" (Faw and Skelton 1986, 194).

Jackie Jackson, Jesse's wife, was also angry and disappointed in her husband's speech. The Jacksons had been asked to sit on the other side of the platform away from the other candidates, and she thought: "Why . . . must we always be the ones to apologize? Why do whites always want that? . . . What is wrong with them? . . . Why are they so relieved? Why were they so fearful? Especially of us? I saw tears and we were confused" (Faw and Skelton 1986, 196).

What Jackson had done was deliver a powerful speech of unification rather than one of castigation as his followers had wanted. Although Jackson's black supporters were cool toward this theme, the effect on the whites was stunning. They were relieved and emotionally overcome. The speech was laced with symbols, references, and themes of national unity.

> Tonight we *come together, bound* by our faith in a mighty God. . . . Leadership must heed the call of conscience—redemption, expansion, healing, and *unity.* . . .
>
> . . . I will be proud to support the nominee of this convention for the presidency of the United States. . . .
>
> I went to see Hubert Humphrey three days before he died. He had just called Richard Nixon from his dying bed, and many people wondered why. . . . What I have concluded is this: when all is said and done, we must support each other, redeem each other, and move on. . . .
>
> America is not like a blanket. . . . It is more like a quilt—many patches, many pieces, many colors, many sizes, all *woven* and *held together* by a *common* thread. The white, the Hispanic, the black, the Arab, the Jew, the woman, the Native American, the small farmer, the businessperson, the environmentalist, the peace activist, the young, the old, the lesbian, the gay, and the disabled make up the American quilt. . . .
>
> . . . We have experienced pain, but progress . . . as we lost Malcolm, Martin, Medgar, Bobby, John, and Viola.
>
> We are *copartners* in a long and rich religious history—the Judeo-Chrisitan traditions. Many blacks and Jews have a *shared* passion for social justice at home and peace abroad. . . . We are *bound* by Moses and Jesus, but also *connected* with Islam and Muhammed. We are *bound* by Dr. Martin Luther King, Jr., and Rabbi Abraham Heschel crying out from their graves for us to reach *common ground.* We are *bound* by *shared* blood and *shared* sacrifices. We are much too intelligent; much too *bound* by our Judeo-Christian heritage . . . to go on divided from one another (Jackson 1984, emphasis added).

The opening part of the speech was in fact a paean to national unity, a theme that any politician with an aspiration to the American presidency must reverberate, especially a minority candidate whose divisiveness is feared. The whites, anticipating retribution, were overcome with the acceptance, forgiveness, and the plea for unity in the speech, while many blacks, anticipating revenge, were bitterly disappointed—at least until they saw the effect the unification theme had on the whites.

The middle of the speech was also unusual in that it was an extended analysis of America's economic condition and the privations imposed on all the poor—a broader theme than the injustices of racism suffered by the blacks. The speech demonstrated that Jackson could handle sophisticated economic issues that embraced the welfare of the entire nation. At the end of the speech he again forged his powerful religious rhetoric. For this one moment in history at least, Jackson had successfully extended his charisma. His time had come.

The 1988 Presidential Campaign

The manuscript for this book was completed before the 1988 presidential primary campaigns began. Now, during the final editing, the April 19 New York primary has just come to its conclusion. Although the New York primary followed the pattern of dynamics outlined in this book, Jesse Jackson's 1988 campaign overall has been rather different from that of 1984. I attribute this to a deliberate and brilliant change in Jackson's strategy: He has followed the unification theme he first adopted in his 1984 Democratic Convention address—and with re markable success. This time he is "running presidential" rather than "running black," and his populist message is garnering white support (Hackett et al. 1988).

His image in the white media has also changed substantially. For example, as the primary campaigns began in Iowa in November 1987, *U.S. News and World Report* saw him, in a cover story entitled "The Man Who Would Be King," as promoting "lunch bucket politics," speaking "crowd-pleasing bromides" to "white faces as far as one can see." Even though it was still said that he could not be nominated, he was described as driving party leaders batty. Some of the old image persisted, as the article went on to say that "modesty is a virtue with which he is not familiar." "Martin had a dream; Jesse had a scheme." And PUSH had become "one of the few ways to gauge his administrative skills" (Kramer 1987, 34–44; Rainie 1987, 41).

After the Super Tuesday primaries, *Newsweek*, in "The Power Broker: What Jesse Jackson Wants" (March 8, 1988), saw a "new Jesse Jackson" with expanded appeal who had "repackaged himself like a punk rocker trying to cross into mainstream pop music." According to *Newsweek*, Jackson "sounded more presidential," "shunned controversy," was "mellowing," and had "real maturity." He was still "charismatic," and *Newsweek* asked, "Is the new Jesse Jackson real?" (Martz et al. 1988, 18–22).

Just before the New York primary on April 19, *Time* still saw him as "populist," "breathtaking," and "demogogic," although by now he could be "eloquent, funny, and provocative." His lack of traditional qualifications had not kept him from changing the Democratic party through his "uncanny ability to invent his own rules and often win by them." On a more negative note, the article stated that Jackson could not "withstand such scrutiny" as his "maladroit stewardship" of PUSH/Excel attested, the program being "a lingering embarrassment" in which the federal agencies "threw money" at him until he and PUSH were "overwhelmed" (Shapiro 1988, 13–22).

Jackson's unification and "economic violence" themes have strong appeal to many whites who are disaffected from the U.S. economic system. He is perceived as a strong and forceful leader, and Democratic voters are evenly split as to whether he would represent all Americans as president—a tremendous improvement over 1984 (*Newsweek* 1988). Most of the time he was careful not to slip into black rhetoric, and he doubled and tripled his percentages of white voters compared to 1984, though he was still far from winning a majority of them. It seemed improbable that he would obtain the Democratic nomination in 1988, but he had demonstrated that he had the capacity to learn about himself and to change his behavior rather dramatically. The critical question still remains as to whose interests he might serve with the power he has obtained.

References

Primary Sources

Amundsen, Father Robert, Catholic clergyman and member, Religious Task Force, Denver. Interview with Eleanor Farrar, Denver, Colorado, 26 May 1981.

Astuno, John, Principal of East High School, Denver. Interview with Ernest R. House, Denver, Colorado, 26 May 1981.

Bates, John, Former teacher and member, Manual Advisory Board, Denver. Interview with Ernest R. House, Denver, Colorado, 27 May 1981.

Berry, Mary Frances, U.S. Commissioiner of Civil Rights, former Assistant Secretary of HEW, and former President, PUSH/Excel Board. Memorandum to Thomas Minter, 2 October 1980.

_____ . Letter to Saundra R. Murray, 17 March 1982a.

_____ . Interview with Ernest R. House, Washington, D.C., 8 July 1982b.

_____ . Letter to Ernest R. House, 30 March 1984.

Biffle, Beverly, Counselor at Manual High School, Denver. Interview with Ernest R. House, Denver, Colorado, 21 May 1981.

Blair, Omar D., President, Denver Board of Education. Interview with Eleanor Farrar, Denver, Colorado, 26 May 1981.

Broussard, Bruce, Chair, Businessmen's Task Group, Denver. Interview with Ernest R. House, Denver, Colorado, 26 May 1981.

Caldwell, Cedric, School liaison at Orchard Knoll, Chattanooga. Interview with Ernest R. House, Chattanooga, Tennessee, 11 June 1981.

Campbell, Lindsay, member, Advisory Council, East High School, Denver. Interview with Ernest R. House, Denver, Colorado, 22 May 1981.

Carey, Rudy, Teacher/advisor at Manual High School, Denver. Interview with Ernest R. House, Denver, Colorado, 26 May 1981.

Cumi, Linda, American Institutes for Research staff. Interview with Eleanor Farrar, Denver, Colorado, 21 May 1981.

Datta, Lois E., Staff, U.S. Office of Education official. Interview with Ernest R. House, Washington, D.C., 8 July 1982.

Dennis, Evie, Denver Public Schools, Director of PUSH/Excel. Interview with Eleanor Farrar, Denver, Colorado, 26 May 1981.

Dixon, Daniel, Illinois Assistant State Superintendent of Education. Memorandum to Joseph M. Cronin, 27 February 1979.

_____ . Interview with Ernest R. House, Champaign, Illinois, 17 October 1983.

Edwards, Betty, Assistant Director of PUSH/Excel, Chattanooga. Interview with Eleanor Farrar, Chattanooga, Tennessee, 11 June 1981.

Farrar, Eleanor. Notes on Meeting of PUSH/Excel Implementation Task Force, Department of Education, Washington, D.C., 24 October 1980.

———. Letter to Elma Mardis, 16 June 1981.

Gee, Mary Joyce, Associate Principal of Howard High School, Chattanooga. Interview with Eleanor Farrar, Chattanooga, Tennessee, 11 June 1981.

Gentile, Mary, Principal, and Vanderlinden, Vice Principal, Manual High School, Denver. Interview with Ernest R. House, Denver, Colorado, 26 May 1981.

Gold, Norman, NIE Program Officer for PUSH/Excel Evaluation. Interview with Eleanor Farrar and Ernest R. House, Washington, D.C., 3 and 4 October 1980a.

———. Interview with Ernest R. House, Chicago, 9 October 1980b.

———. Telephone conversation with Eleanor Farrar, 13 May 1981.

———. Meeting with Eleanor Farrar, Washington, D.C., 7 January 1982a.

———. Interview with Ernest R. House, Washington, D.C., 8 July 1982b.

Gold, Norman, and Moses, Kathlyn. Meeting with Eleanor Farrar, Washington, D.C., 7 January 1982.

Graham, Patricia A., Dean, Harvard School of Education, and former Director of the National Institute of Education. Interview with Robert Stake and Eleanor Farrar, Cambridge, Massachusetts, 18 June 1981.

Hamilton, Paul, Former coordinator of PUSH/Excel. Interview with Ernest R. House, Denver, Colorado, 21 May 1981.

Hendrix, Clifford, Assistant Superintendent, Chattanooga Schools. Interview with Ernest R. House, Chattanooga, Tennessee, 11 June 1981.

Houghtaling, Dianne, Teacher/advisor at East High School, Denver. Interview with Ernest R. House, Denver, Colorado, 26 May 1981.

Lee, Ann, AIR site data collector, Denver. Interview with Ernest R. House, Denver, Colorado, 27 May 1981.

Mardis, Elma H., National Director of PUSH for Excellence. Interview with Ernest R. House, Chattanooga, Tennessee, 12 June 1981.

———. Letter to Saundra R. Murray, 23 April 1982.

Murray, Charles A., Former Chief Scentist, American Institutes for Research. Interview with Eleanor Farrar, Washington, D.C., 17 December 1980.

———. Interview with Eleanor Farrar and Ernest R. House, Washington, D.C., 9 July 1982a.

———. Letter to Ernest R. House, 13 July 1982b.

———. Letter to Norman Gold, 23 October 1982c.

Murray, Saundra R., PUSH/Excel Evaluation Project Director. Interview with Eleanor Farrar, AIR, Washington, D.C., 2 October 1980.

———. Interview with Eleanor Farrar, Washington, D.C., 7 January 1982a.

———. Interview with Eleanor Farrar, Huron Institute, Cambridge, Massachusetts, 12 April 1982b.

Prescott, Phyllis, President, Denver Parent Teachers Association. Interview with Ernest R. House, Denver, Colorado, 26 May 1981.

Radefsky, Martha, Member, Central Fund-raising Committee, Denver. Interview with Ernest R. House, Denver, Colorado, 27 May 1981.

Rich, Spencer. Reporter, *Washington Post*. Telephone conversation with Eleanor Farrar, July 1982.

Richardson, Cordell, PUSH/Excel Western Regional Director. Letter to Saundra R. Murray, 23 July 1979.

Rossi, Peter, Director, Social and Demographic Research Institute, University of Massachusetts. Letter to Norman Gold, 23 July 1979.

Schiller, Jeffrey, and Stalford, Charles, National Institute of Education officials. Interview with Eleanor Farrar and Ernest R. House, Washington, D.C., 8 July 1982.

Schwarz, Paul, President, American Institutes for Research. Interview with Eleanor Farrar and Ernest R. House, AIR, Washington, D.C., 19 July 1982.

Smith, Carol, University of Illinois data collector. Report on PUSH-Excel Retreat on 19–20 June 1980. July 1980.

Smith, Linda M., AIR site data collector, Chattanooga. Interview with Eleanor Farrar, Chattanooga, Tennessee, 12 June 1981.

──── . Field Notes: Stakeholder Meeting, Chattanooga, Tennessee, 23 March 1982.

Smith, Willard, Coordinator of Denver PUSH/Excel. Interview with Ernest R. House, Denver, Colorado, 25 and 26 May 1981.

Walker, Malcolm, School District Coordinator, Chattanooga PUSH/Excel. Interview with Eleanor Farrar, Chattanooga, Tennessee, 12 June 1981.

Warfield, Charles, PUSH Director of Operations. Interview with Ernest R. House, Kalamazoo, Michigan, October 1980.

Welsh, Michael, PUSH/Excel Community Liaison, Denver. Interview with Eleanor Farrar and Ernest R. House, Denver, Colorado, 26 May 1981.

Witherspoon, John, Chattanooga Chamber of Commerce and PUSH/Excel Advisory Board Member. Interview with Ernest R. House, Chattanooga, Tennessee, 11 June 1981.

Wortman, Paul M., Codirector, Methodology and Evaluation Research, Northwestern University. "Comments on the AIR Draft Evaluation Design of the Push for Excellence Program," mimeo, 30 July 1979.

Secondary Sources

Abernathy, Ralph David. 1985. "Foreword." In Thomas Landess and Richard Quinn, *Jesse Jackson and the Politics of Race*. Ottawa, Illinois: Jameson.

American Institutes for Research. 1978. *Evaluation of Project EXCEL: Technical Proposal*. In response to RFP: NIE-R-78-0026. October. Washington, D.C.: AIR.

──── . 1979. *National Evaluation of the PUSH for Excellence Project: Phase I: Program Description*. July. Washington, D.C.: AIR.

──── . 1980. *Annual Report 1980*. Washington, D.C.: AIR.

Babcock, Charles R. 1988a. "Jackson's Record as Manager." *Washington Post*, April 10, p. 1.

————. 1988b. "Jackson's Personal Income Up Since '84 Campaign." *Washington Post*, April 10, p. A14.

Bendix, Reinhart. 1962. *Max Weber: An Intellectual Portrait*. New York: Doubleday.

Branscombe, Art. 1979. "'Sermon' by Jackson Opens PUSH/Excel." *Denver Post*, September 12, p. 20.

Brimmer, Andrew F. 1987. "Income and Wealth." *Ebony*, August, 42, no. 10, pp. 42–48.

Brown, Frank Dexter. 1983. "Jesse Jackson's Push for Power." *Black Enterprise*, November, pp. 46–54.

Burton, Thomas M. 1987. "PUSH Unit Owes $1 million in Misspent Funds to U.S." *Chicago Tribune*, June 21, section 2, pp. 1–2.

Califano, Joseph A., Jr. 1981. *Governing America*. New York: Simon and Schuster.

Canetti, Elias. 1960. *Crowds and Power*. New York: Continuance.

Champaign-Urbana News-Gazette. 1983. "Stroh's Buys Ads to Squelch Rumors." December 11, p. H-1.

Chicago Tribune. 1983a. "PUSH: Jackson's Candidacy Focuses Attention on Operation PUSH." November 6, section 6, p. 7.

————. 1983b. "PUSH-Excel Gets Low Grades." December 28, p. 1.

Comer, James P. 1987. "Education Is the Way Out and Up." *Ebony*, August, 42, no. 10, pp. 61–66.

Curry, George E. 1982. "Complex Issues Cloud Busch Boycott Rift." *St. Louis Post-Dispatch*, August 22, pp. 1F, 6F.

Denver Post. 1981a. "PUSH/Excel Program Hasn't Worked—Study." May 1, p. 2.

————. 1981b. "PUSH/Excel Head Says Denver Program Different." May 5, p. 3.

Drotning, Paul T., and South, W. W. 1970. "Jesse Jackson: The 'Now' Look in Religion." In *Up from the Ghetto*. New York: Cowles, pp. 19–43.

Ebony. 1987. "The New Black Middle Class." August 42, no. 10.

Farrar, Eleanor, and House, Ernest R. 1983. "The Evaluation of PUSH/Excel: A Case Study." *New Directions for Program Evaluation* 17, pp. 5–25. Reprinted in E. R. House (ed.), *New Directions for Educational Evaluation*. Lewes, Sussex, and Philadelphia: Falmer Press, 1986.

Faw, Bob, and Skelton, Nancy. 1986. *Thunder in America*. Austin, Texas: Texas Monthly Press.

Frazier, E. Franklin. 1963. *The Negro Church in America*. New York: Schocken Books.

Frazier, Regina Jollivette. 1987. "Is the Black Middle Class Blowing It? No!" *Ebony*, August, 42, no. 10, pp. 89–90.

Fullan, Michael. 1982. *The Meaning of Educational Change*. New York: Teachers College Press.

Geertz, Clifford. 1983. *Local Knowledge: Further Essays in Interpretative Anthropology*. New York: Basic Books.

Glazer, Nathan, and Moynihan, Daniel Patrick. 1963. *Beyond the Melting Pot*. Cambridge: The M.I.T. Press.

Gold, Norman. 1981. *The Stakeholder Process in Educational Program Evaluation*. Washington, D.C.: NIE.

Hackett, George, with Karen Springen, Ginny Carroll, and Howard Fineman. 1988. "Jackson's White Vote." *Newsweek*, April 11, pp. 28–29.

Hare, Nathan. 1987. "Is the Black Middle Class Blowing It? Yes!" *Ebony*, August, 42, no. 10.

Harper's. 1986. "What Does Government Owe the Poor?" April, pp. 35–47.

Hill, Robert B. 1987. "The Black Middle Class Defined." *Ebony*, August, 42, no. 10.

Hodgson, Godfrey. 1976. *America in Our Time*. New York: Vintage.

House, Ernest R. 1974. *The Politics of Educational Innovation*. Berkeley, California: McCutchan.

———. 1983. "How We Think About Evaluation." In E. House (ed.) *Philosophy of Evaluation*, New Directions for Program Evaluation, 19. San Francisco: Jossey Bass, pp. 5–25. Reprinted in Ross Conners et al., *Evaluation Studies Review Annual* 9. Beverly Hills, California: 1984.

House, Ernest R., and Madura, William. 1987. *Race, Gender and Jobs*. Boulder: Laboratory for Policy Studies, University of Colorado.

Huberman, A. Michael, and Miles, Matthew B. 1984. *Innovation Up Close: How School Improvement Works*. New York: Plenum.

Hurston, Zora Neale. 1983. *The Sanctified Church*. Berkeley, California: Turtle Island.

Hughes, Everett, et al., 1950. *Race and Culture*, vol. 1 of *The Collected Papers of Robert E. Park*. Glencoe, Illinois: Free Press.

Isaacson, Walter. 1983. "Seeking Votes and Clout." *time*, August 22, pp. 19–31.

Jackson, Rev. Jesse L. 1977. "Victim-Victimizer: Why Excel?" In Rev. Jesse Jackson, *Straight from the Heart*. Washington, D.C.: Fortress, 1987.

———. 1978. "Save Our Children: Administrators for Excellence." In Rev. Jesse Jackson, *Straight from the Heart*. Washington, D.C.: Fortress, 1987.

———. 1979. "An Appeal and a Challenge to Sears to Withdraw the Suit: *Sears vs. the U.S. Government*." Chicago: PUSH, Inc.

———. 1984a. "The Candidates Challenge: The Call of Conscience, the Courage of Conviction." In Rev. Jesse Jackson, *Straight from the Heart*. Washington, D.C.: Fortress, 1987.

———. 1984b. "The Rainbow Coalition." Chicago: Jesse Jackson for President Committee.

———. 1984c. Speech to the Democratic National Convention, San Francisco, July 17.

———. 1987. *Straight from the Heart*. Washington, D.C.: Fortress.

Jarrett, Vernon. 1983. "Jackson's Bid Spawns False Litmus Test." *Chicago Sun-Times*, November 6, p. 8.

Johnson, Dirk, and Mitchell, Dick. 1983. "What Makes Jesse Run?" *Sunday Sun-Times*, October 30, pp. 1, 4.

Joyce, Fay S. 1983. "Presidential Decision Nears for Jesse Jackson." *The New York Times*, September 22, pp. 1, 13.

Kilson, Martin. 1971. "Black Politicians: A New Power." *Dissent*, August, pp. 333–345.

Kramer, Michael. 1987. "What to Make of the New Jesse." *U.S. News and World Report*, November 16, pp. 34–44.

Landess, Thomas, and Quinn, Richard. 1985. *Jesse Jackson and the Politics of Race.* Ottawa, Illinois: Jameson Books.

Landry, Bart. 1987. *The New Black Middle Class.* Berkeley, California: University of California Press.

Lowi, Theodore. 1971. *The Politics of Disorder.* New York: Basic Books.

Majors, Richard. 1983. "The Press Reaction in the 1983 Chicago Mayoral Campaign." University of Illinois, College of Education, unpublished paper.

Martz, Larry, with Harold Fineman, Sylvester Monroe, Eleanor Clift, and Andrew Murr. 1988. "The Power Broker: What Jesse Jackson Wants." *Newsweek,* March 21, pp. 18–22.

McMillan, George. 1976. *The Making of an Assassin: The Life of James Earl Ray.* Boston: Little Brown.

Mills, Sylvia J. 1980. "PUSH/Excel: What Is Its Worth?" *Chicago Defender,* April 26, p. 1.

Morganthau, Tom, with Monroe, Sylvester. 1981. "Jesse Jackson's Troubles." *Time,* July 20, p. 29.

Morganthau, Tom, et al. 1983. "What Makes Jesse Run?" *Newsweek,* November 14, pp. 49–52, 54–56.

Murray, Charles. 1984. *Losing Ground: American Social Policy, 1950–1980.* New York: Basic Books.

Murray, Saundra R., and Murray, Charles A., et al. 1979. *The National Evaluation of the PUSH for Excellence Project: Phase I: Evaluation Design.* July. Washington D.C.: AIR.

———. 1980. *The National Evaluation of the PUSH for Excellence Project: Technical Report 1: The Evolution of a Program.* March. Washington, D.C.: AIR.

Murray, Saundra R., and Thompkins, Nadine. 1979. *The National Evaluation of the PUSH for Excellence Project: Phase I: Assessment of Stakeholders Needs.* July. Washington, D.C.: AIR.

Murray, Saundra R., et al. 1980. *The National Evaluation of the PUSH for Excellence Project: Technical Report 2: Implementation.* November. Washington, D.C.: AIR.

———. 1981. *The National Evaluation of the PUSH for Excellence Project: Technical Report 3: The Program, the School and the Students.* April. Washington, D.C.: AIR.

———. 1982. *The National Evaluation of the PUSH for Excellence Project: Final Report.* March. Washington, D.C.: AIR.

Myrdal, Gunnar. 1944. *An American Dilemma: The Negro Problem and Modern Democracy.* New York: Harper and Row.

National Institute of Education. 1978. "Request for Proposal NIE-R-78-0026. Evaluation of Project Excel." September 5. *Newsweek.* 1988. "Rating Jesse: A Newsweek Poll." April 11, p. 29.

New York Times. 1983a. "Jackson Hints at a Decision Soon About '84 as He Takes Time Off." September 26.

———. 1983b. "Do You Believe That Any Jew Should Support This Man? Should Any Decent American?" November 11.

Oates, S. B. 1982. *Let the Trumpets Sound.* New York: New American Library.

Omi, Michael, and Winant, Howard. 1986. *Racial Formation in the United States.* New York and London: Routledge, Kegan, Paul.

Among the projects which received donations from
The Elsa Wild Animal Appeal and Elsa Trust from 1962 to 1977

		£
Samburu County Council	Establish Game Reserve	7,000
Game Department	Trapping and Poaching Control Officer	11,400
E. A. Wildlife Society	Game Rescue Team	9,000
National Park Game Wardens	Flying Tuition	1,750
Meru County Council	Establishing Game Reserve	15,418
G. Adamson	Born Free Lion Rehabilitation	2,042
E. A. Wildlife Society	Rothschild Giraffe Translocation	1,350
Elsa Wild Animal Appeal, USA	Establishment of USA Elsa Corporation	15,609
Tuber Productions	Animal Ark TV Pilot Film	2,450
Oxford University Expedition	Sitatungu Research Cherangani	670
Tsavo National Park	Fire Breaks	728
Shimba Hill National Park	Warden's House	4,210
Falkland Islands Expedition	Bird Research	50
Wildlife Clubs of Kenya	Publications, Administration Expenses	24,162
A. Hurxthal	Ostrich Research	1,432
Oxford University Expedition	Red Colobus Research, Zanzibar	400
Nairobi National Park	Veterinary Aid Fund	244
Nairobi National Park	Education Booklets	776
Kenya Rifles Officers' Safari Club	Land Rover	2,682
Tana River Council, Kora Game Reserve	Tractor Trailer	4,800
Shaba Game Reserve, Isiolo County Council	Toyota	2,000
Shaba Game Reserve, Isiolo County Council	Airstrip	300
Thailand	Sunday Market in Bangkok	1,000

Donations may be sent to:

The Elsa Wild Animal
Appeal,
c/o The Charities Aid Fund,
48 Pembury Road,
Tonbridge,
Kent. England

The Elsa Wild Animal
Appeal,
P.O. Box 864,
Station K,
Toronto,
Ontario M4P 2H2. Canada